Self-Power Is the Great I Am

Empirical

Volume I

Jybe Yvves

ISBN 978-1-0980-3387-3 (paperback)
ISBN 978-1-0980-3389-7 (digital)

Copyright © 2020 by Jybe Yvves

All rights reserved. No part of this publication may be reproduced, distributed, or transmitted in any form or by any means, including photocopying, recording, or other electronic or mechanical methods without the prior written permission of the publisher. For permission requests, solicit the publisher via the address below.

Christian Faith Publishing, Inc.
832 Park Avenue
Meadville, PA 16335
www.christianfaithpublishing.com

All scriptures, unless otherwise stated, are taken from the King James Version of the Holy Bible.

Printed in the United States of America

I dedicate this book to my loving and amazing husband, Joshua, and two beautiful daughters, Satori and Selah. You are my heart. To my mother, Mari Rose, who is in my heart, and my brother, Austin, who I love dearly. To my God who constantly creates me, calls me, loves me, keeps me, and strengthens me. I am forever in love with You. To You be all the glory, honor, and praise.

1

God Proves Himself with Science

The wonderful thing about God is that He's not in an uproar over what His creation believes or doesn't believe. He knows that He's solid. That is why He is called the solid rock in which we stand countless times in the oldest most proven book today. Deuteronomy 32:4 said, "The Rock, his work is perfect, for all his ways are justice. A God of faithfulness and without iniquity, just and upright is he."

Science, including neuroscientists, use the wisdom, truth, and knowledge that God has left us with. Yes, in this current year, 2019, they are proving God's written Word. Little do they know that it is God both acting and willing in them to accomplish His great purpose. In Philippians 2:13, it said, "For it is God who works in you to will and to act in order to fulfill His good purpose or to do of His good pleasure." And Proverbs 30:5 said, "Every word of God proves true," and yes, scientifically. What these scientists need to realize is that they were formed by God and that wonderful brain too, and it is God that is giving them the wisdom and revelation to prove these already existing truths that have been around since the beginning of time.

James 1:5 tells us that if we ask for wisdom, God will give it generously without finding fault: "If any of you lacks wisdom, he should ask God, who gives generously to all without finding fault, and it will be given to him." You may say, "Well, Jybe, scientists didn't ask for wisdom. They just have it…" Wrong.

In the last days, God says, "I will pour out My Spirit on all people. Your sons and daughters will prophesy. Your young men will see visions. Your old men will dream dreams." God is saying here that you don't even need to be a professing Christian to have His Spirit working in you! Remember that scripture that specifies that it is God that is both acting and willing in an individual to accomplish His great purpose or of His good pleasure! Didn't He harden the Pharaoh's heart? Yes! The Pharaoh was clearly not a professing Christian.

See, God can use wicked people to shame them and show off His powerful wraths against them. God knows who will serve Him and those that just want to remain evil. He will just encourage them in the way they want to stay in to benefit His sons and daughters, clearly what He did here and what He is doing with science. God needs people that are chasing after a new discovery that is of a good purpose, people that have a seeking heart for truth and discovery with an innocent heart. God is able to shower that person with success in knowledge and wisdom because these things affect mankind.

When it comes to evil people that are trying to harm others or are harming others, the difficult thing is that they are of a depraved mind and they hinder God from working in them for positivity. God can only work with what the individual is releasing from their heart. So if a person that may be neutral or undecided in their hearts, God can encourage them in the right way. Now if their of a depraved mind, He has to work around it, and He will work all things out for the good (Romans 8:28).

Some people think that God made the Pharaoh hard in his heart all by Himself when that is not the case! The Pharaoh was evil way before God showed up here. That's why God had to get involved in the first place. God had a greater picture here by making sure the Pharaoh's heart stayed the way it did. God was making sure that the Pharaoh paid for all of his sins! God knew this man's inner repetitiveness addiction to power and control would be fickle. God is the righteous Judge and an angry Father when He needs to be! He wanted to make the Egyptians pay for all that they did to His people. God has laws in place, and when there's someone like the Pharaoh that has monstrous charges against himself, that righteous Judge is coming!

Self-Power Is the Great I Am

When you have the Pharaoh that is not stronger than God and thinks that he is, you better believe that they woke up the Lion of the Tribe Of Judah. And God very boss-like handled the Pharaoh like a toy that he was! So even if the Pharaoh was kind for a bit, he would ultimately turn hard again… Why? Because the Pharaoh served false gods that had no power and were blatantly against God Jehovah. If you serve corrupt and evil false gods, then so are you. So the Pharaoh was a hopeless disaster before God showed up.

Put it this way: God wasn't there to show loving kindness and mercy toward Egypt. He was there to show His wrath and revenge and vengeance! He had hatred toward Egypt, and He was going to make them suffer and pay for all that they did! So people want to have compassion to a serial killer and psychopath that was never going to change. Like the Pharaoh, you're a joke! I have to say that my Dad, great God Jehovah, makes any notorious imbecile look like a dried-up worm.

See, God talks about several kinds of people. There are three that I will talk on right now: the Christian, the children of God; the depraved, the children of Satan; and the lost or orphaned that are in the unknown and just searching for the truth. Well, scientists do mostly that; they are constantly proving to get down to the truth. So you better believe that God will be blessing them with favor in successful breakthroughs on all categories because it all concerns Him. Science is proving humanity, creation, matter, and universe in such a miraculous or supernatural way.

Doctors are in the business of healing people and caring for people, so also know that God is blessing them with wisdom because it concerns mankind and aiding to His creation in living a long life.

If individuals believe that we just happened to be this phenomenal of a creature—spiritually, mentally, physically, infinitely, and eternally by accident—I confidently say you are pitifully wrong. Science has already proven God over and over. God loves His creation so much that He has heard the cries of those that have said, "I have to see to believe." Remember what He did for Thomas the apostle, or do you not know that He proved Himself for Thomas?

Jybe Yvves

Thomas, an apostle of Jesus Himself, said, "I have to see to believe. I have to place my fingers in the wounds where He was pierced!" Jesus said that blessed are those who don't need to see to believe, but He will bless those that need to see to believe even in our modern day.

I have two daughters, one five years of age and the other is almost two. My love for them is infinitely unchangeable. I know that if one of my daughters were experiencing a difficult time learning a topic more than the other, I would be patient and go to great lengths to teach her. God, being the wonderful Father that He is, has also gone to great lengths to teach us. Please know that He has been progressively giving mankind wisdom to prove His Word true, especially for the ones that need to see in order to believe.

An atheist will claim that they have self-power, and this statement is hilarious coming from someone that is so sure that there is no God. To have true self-power, you must put into action all of God's words. They must understand that God's Word is God Himself. John 1:1 said, "In the beginning the Word already existed. The word was with God and the word was God." And John 1:3 said, "Through Him things were made; without Him nothing was made that has been made."

Side note: If atheists think we came from nothing, then nothing should exist! If atheists think that no one created us, then no one should be able to create. These statements are jaw-droppingly insane! So if the rituals that one is performing to manifest self-power, they are taking God's instructions to a better life and having it without the fullness of what else He has to offer.

Atheism or any religion that opposes God is in fact so close to God that they are blinder than a bat to not see God. I say this with much love; however, self-power is obtained on what God has instructed us to do as mankind. Now if more of the faith-based Christians would truly operate in self-power, they would see God's promises come to pass. God gifted mankind with self-power. Let me elaborate. The parents of a child understand that they are the ones with full power, but by all means, they need their child to pick up that spoon and eat for themselves. Eventually, the child must learn to shower, use restroom on their own, and let alone think for themselves. Don't you think God needs you to take care of your own business, life, thoughts, and so on? Dare I say, your own healing, meditation, and imaginations?

Christianity is not being lazy. It's powerful. It's a work. It's a duty. Think I'm wrong? Let me prove it to you that I'm not. God calls us kings in the earth many times throughout the Bible, especially in the book of Revelation. He's the King of kings and we're sons and daughters of the Most High God. He commands us to take every thought captive and to bring it into the obedience of Jesus Christ. He wouldn't command us if we had no power to do so! When we ask our children to do something, we know that they are able to do so. So when God commands us to not be fearful and to have great courage, we're able to. When He commands us to be full of joy instead of sorrow, we're able to. In order to do what God asks us to do, we must have self-power. We must have mind control. Christians have gotten so confused on self-power, and the sad thing is that they have rendered themselves powerless because of it. Jesus said greater works will we be doing than the works He has done. Christians wait for God to gust power through them which mostly never happens unless you have been praying and meditating or seriously channeling your God-given power.

So many Christians have wasted their life powerless and have thought that God dealt them a bad deck of cards in their life. You must understand that when you confessed Jesus as your Lord and Savior, you are now in Christ, so anything that you do is actually in Christ. So to have self-power as a Christian, we have it to the fullest because we're in Christ Jesus, and we acknowledge that we have self-power because we are made in the image of God. In fact, we have greater riches in the spirit than someone who is operating in their self-power without acknowledging God. All of mankind are made in the image of God and all of mankind have self-power just by being human!! Christians have thought that God does everything for us, absolutely everything, to calm our mind and fears down, our sicknesses to go away, and the list goes on. When we are left with no change in our lives, we blame God and take no responsibility for the things that we are entirely able to change. If you're tired of living a certain way, stop living that way!

I remember there was a time that I dealt with an unpeaceful mind for two years straight. The medical field would have put me on medication. However, I experienced God and gave my life to Him with all the knowledge of the Word of God. I still wasn't experiencing peace. I was depressed and fearful all the time. I refused any medicine knowing that it would only have a list of side effects I couldn't handle. I remember crying out in my spirit to God. These were my words... "When are you going to take this away, God?"

He said, "I already did!" But He shouted it through me like He was fed up with me and that got my attention. However, I remember telling God that I'm tired of being so fearful and depressed.

He said, "Then stop it." I didn't quite understand how I could just stop feeling like this, but now looking back on it, He's saying that I can stop it because I have the mind control to do so.

I remember I was helping my church at the time in Fresno, California. I was doing the media for youth worship that night. I was experiencing these tormenting thoughts I could not shake. And while worship was going on, I had a mental vision or imagination of God on the throne and this shriveled hairless white demon that was covering his face was sitting at the feet of God. God then asked me how come I didn't live a life of peace. My response was not verbal but with body language. I used my hands and aimed them at the demon. It was a pure lightbulb that illuminated in me in that moment, nine years ago, that changed me forever when I was using my hands to point out the demon as the one to blame instead of my words. That was me subconsciously fearful that I would never change this fearful thinking and subconsciously more fearful of the enemy than really believing in God that I'm no longer subject to this fearful thinking.

God would whisper in my heart, "You're choosing the very thing that you're fighting." He explained that by me being so terrified that I may never have a healthy mental state was in fact the way that I was choosing this dark matter, demonic lie, and stronghold that God says for us to take captive and to bring into His obedience.

Self-Power Is the Great I Am

To bring that thought into God's obedience means to take that thought or cluster of thoughts known as strongholds to make them submit and comply to His authority and truth. God also whispered into my heart and said, "Your thoughts are lovely, just, pure, and of good report. You actually have My mind."

We are given the mind of Christ when we confess Him as our Lord and Savior. My response in my heart would be, "How though, Lord? Because all my thoughts have been so awful!"

He said, "You're being framed and blamed for those negative thoughts." God calls Satan as the accuser of the brethren. These are false accusations that frame a person so perfectly that they must be guilty, right? The thing is that it's a false accusation!! Long story short, just because you have a thought, it doesn't mean it's yours. God calls them fiery darts of the enemy, trickery of the enemy. He will place thoughts and then accuse you of them.

> Put on the full armor of God, so that you can take your stand against the devil's schemes. For our struggle is not against flesh and blood, but against the rulers, against the authorities, against the powers of this dark world and against the spiritual forces of evil in the heavenly realms. Therefore put on the full armor of God, so that when the day of evil comes, you may be able to stand your ground, and after you have done everything, to stand. Stand firm then, with the belt of truth buckled around your waist, with the breastplate of righteousness in place, and with your feet fitted with the readiness that comes from the gospel of peace. In addition to all this, take up the shield of faith, with which you can extinguish all the flaming arrows of the evil one. Take the helmet of salvation and the sword of the Spirit, which is the word of God. (Ephesians 6:11–17)

Keep in mind that the day of evil could be any dark day you come across; however, be ready mentally!

Beware of the wiles of the enemy. Remember when Jesus was being tempted in the desert? The Gospels of Matthew, Mark, and Luke discuss this moment. In this day and age, our medical diagnosis for Jesus would most likely be hallucinating due to malnourishment and some have said schizophrenia. I have to say I don't argue with that diagnosis. Doctors have to give a name to a symptom that a patient is dealing with; however, God has called these things not a health problem but a demonic warfare. We don't see Jesus got worried about a demonic experience, yet He very well understands that this dark world exist. And in order to get it under control is not to throw medicine at it or to fear it, but to use the Word of God and to be afraid of it is absolutely silly. A drug doesn't heal you; it intoxicates your brain. Instead, you must search within yourself to release your power that you've been given to stop the fear.

Along with great nutrition, please notice that in the following scripture in Matthew, Jesus was fasting and extremely malnourished! Please don't miss that Jesus is proving that the lack of nutrition is definitely playing a key part in this demonic experience. See when God blessed mankind, He thoroughly provided for us and kept us far from evil, even seeing it or completely separate from the unseen world.

God gave us every seed that produces our fruits and vegetables, and He gave us livestock with springs of water to stay alive and thrive! He gave us our sunlight that is loaded with vitamin D which is really essential to prevent hallucinations in people who deal with schizophrenia and depression, same with folate/folic acid also known as Vitamin B9, aids in being happy and nutritionally balanced. Look at the nutrition as God's glorious shield protecting us from mental illness also known as demonic warfare, disease, or the curse. Revelation 22:1 said, "Then the angel showed me a river with the water of life, clear as crystal, flowing from the throne of God and of the Lamb." It flowed down the center of the main street. On each side of the river grew a tree of life, bearing twelve crops of fruit with a fresh crop each month. The leaves were used for medicine to heal the nations.

> Then Jesus was lead by the Spirit into the wilderness to be tempted by the devil. After fasting forty days and forty nights, He was hungry. The tempter came to Him and said, "If you are the Son of God, tell these stones to become bread." Holy Spirit has a presence or frequency of peace that is God's stamp above all else let the Spirit of peace empire or rule your heart. The enemy has a presence or frequency of confusion, forcefulness, anxiety, panic etc. Knowing your Father's voice is absolutely essential! Both have vibrations now discern if it is God or the deceiver.
>
> Jesus answered, "It is written: 'Man shall not live on bread alone, but on every word that comes from the mouth of God.' Then the devil took Him to the holy city and had Him stand on the highest point of the temple. "If you are the Son of God," He said, "throw yourself down. For it is written: 'He will command His angels concerning you, and they will lift you up with their hands, So that you will not strike your foot against a stone. Jesus answered Him.' It is also written: 'Do not put your Lord God to the test.' Again the devil took Him to a very high mountain and showed Him all the kingdoms of the world and their splendor. "All this I will give you," he said, "if you will bow down and worship me." Jesus said, "Away from me Satan! For it is written: 'Worship the Lord your God, and serve Him only.'" Then the devil left Him, and angels came and attended Him. (Matthew 4:1–11)

Let me point out some very important things here and to some weak people in the faith that this would be very frightening to. If Jesus were to check Himself into a local hospital in this day and era and tell doctors what the scripture just said, they would think Jesus was losing His mind. If He told them that Satan made Him stand on the highest building and told Him to jump off it, doctors would say He is mentally ill and suicidal. But in fact, the Bible clearly specifies an evil world with demonic powers are in existence. There have been endless cases of people with absurd stories that are dismissed as mentally ill and never told that it's in fact demonic warfare that they have power over! Jesus became so emptied of Himself that He was able to see in a realm that did in fact exist. A very important fact to point out is that Jesus did not let fear overcome Him. To encourage anyone that may have a fear of mental illness or PTSD, stop being afraid. Identify that it's not you. You're not crazy. You can make it stop by understanding that it is a powerless evil that only when you fear it, you actually ignite it. We can create the most fearsome fires, right? But we have to put the flame to something to set it ablaze. Don't set your energy in fearful imaginations and feelings that will cause a vicious fire. Control your thinking! There's no monster under the bed! There's no lion out in the road! The sky is not falling!

Understand that realms exist! Understand that Jesus taught about kingdoms, dominions, and powers of the unseen world. This is why He commands us to not consult witches and those that practice divination by demonic sources such as fortune-telling. The power of belief is what makes the so-called prediction of your future come to pass. God doesn't want your powerful belief to cause something that is untrue or harmful to manifest in your life, so He is protecting us from lies that are created by wicked people. Look at what happened to King Saul when he consulted demonic forces that lied to him and caused the actual thing she spoke to manifest very quickly in his life because he was so distraught, fragile, and easy to believe anything, and he did!

Please read 1 Samuel 28: 3–25. When you become mature and advanced in the faith of God and the things of God, you are made resilient that even the demonic world recognizes your power and authority. The demons in Acts 19:15 said, "Jesus, I know, and Paul I know. But who are you?" When you become advanced and produce a rare, authentic kind of faith and relationship with God by operating in your God-given self-power, you are a force to be reckoned with for the kingdom of God! The enemy can no longer toy with you, and your mind is not a playground. You create order and run the realms of your thoughts, consciousness, subconsciousness, imaginations, and the meditations of your heart.

John 14:30 said, "Satan can find nothing in me. He has no power over me." This scripture applies to you when you're no longer weak and an infant in the faith. Where you use to trip up and fall, you won't anymore, and he can't slap you around with confusion and fear or with your weaknesses any longer. But you need to stop it! You need to take responsibility. It doesn't matter what isn't fair. It doesn't matter who hurt you. It happened, and now you're left with you. Just because a kingdom is in shambles, it doesn't mean that it isn't a kingdom. Clean up the mess! Just because you didn't make the mess, clean it up! Stop telling your sob story; it's pitiful! And guess what? It paralyzes you! God doesn't want you chasing after everyone's sympathy! Okay, something awful happened, and it happened. Now it's time to heal. Let it go! God has everything that you lost. He has anyone that you lost. He will deal with anyone who caused you trouble! Now stop being a broken record! Don't you remember Jezebel pitied her husband, Ahab, who was weak and always operating in self-pity. It's *pathetic*! Moving on!

God talks about the blessing and the curse that coexist!

> When the Lord your God has brought you into the land you are entering to possess, you are to proclaim on Mount Gerizim the blessings, and on Mount Ebal the curses. (Deuteronomy 11:29)

God is making clear that two worlds exist as clear as the two mountains! You can operate in a world that is so real of negativity or a world so real of positivity. God's abundance is at your fingertips right now; just change you. The very real negative world exist as well. A curse that is so real that is co-existing simultaneously with the blessing of abundant life. You have the power to choose! Deuteronomy 11:26 said, "Look today I am giving you the choice between a blessing and a curse! You will be blessed if you obey the commands of the Lord your God that I am giving you today!" But you will be cursed if you reject the commands of the Lord your God and turn away from Him and the way that He commanded of you today by following other gods, which you have not known. So create your own reality! God is telling you to choose!!!!

Neuroscience is proving meditation to be very real and the spiritual can in fact change the physical or quantum world. Then once again, science is proving the Word of God. Science has actually been proving that thoughts create reality, which the Bible has always said. As a person thinks, so are they (Proverbs 23:7). What they need to understand is that thoughts also create an unseen demonic world that can have effects of mental illness. They can also show us the brain scan of a mentally depressed person versus a brain scan of a mentally healthy individual. A form of dark matter I say is entirely present. The whole brain looks cloudy and dark while the other healthy brain is literally illuminated like it has lights all turned on.

God is called the Father of lights and specifies that our minds are like His. In John 8:12 again, Jesus spoke to them, saying, "I am the light of the world. Whoever follows me will not walk in darkness, but will have the light of life!" Can we agree that the brain that looks like it's seriously lit up with lights is a healthy brain and that individual is mentally healthy and thriving? Who knows if this individual is a professing Christian? But let's acknowledge that God has said that He has poured out His spirit on all flesh, all flesh, on every breathing human being—the just and unjust.

We have Christians who are depressed. Some have even been pastors who committed suicide. Even myself, I was speaking in tongues and still expecting God to heal me, when in fact, He already did, and I was believing a false accusation against me and giving attention to lies that really have nothing to do with me a.k.a. fiery darts. We must work out our own salvation with fear and trembling. This scripture just means get it! Work it out. You got this. Stop being

Self-Power Is the Great I Am

silly and afraid and giving power to a stripped enemy who trembles at the name of our God! You're incredibly powerful! Are you going to argue with me then? Because you can have an unbeliever with a healthy body and a Christian with a sick one and vice versa. It goes to show us that it has everything to do with self-power and mind control that all have access to this God-given self-power. It's your loss if you don't understand that God says that in all you're getting, get understanding! Proverbs 4:7 said, "Wisdom is the principal thing; therefore get wisdom: and with all thy getting get understanding!"

In 1 Thessalonians 5:5, it said, "You are all children of the light and children of the day. You do not belong to the night or the darkness." I believe this scripture is talking to mankind, sinners, and all faith-based tribes and clans and all different types of religions including Satanists. This scripture is stating that every single human is made for light and not for darkness. We can't live in it very long. Our bodies begin to physically break down. All other religions have no leader that states that they are the creator or savior of mankind, let alone no other false god or Satan has given their own life up for humanity and to humanity and in front of humanity so that it could be recorded in history for mankind.

What we see in the brain scans or body scans that show dark cloudy images, I believe, is the darkness the scripture God says that we are not made for because we will surely perish in it. Physically, we will die. All wages of sin, meaning missing the mark is death. As a person thinks in their heart, so are they (Proverbs 23:7). Can we agree that what reflects in that medical image reveals what we have been thinking like and just because we love God we can certainly not be obeying Him? Obeying Him to the point to where our bodies and mind are physically breaking down because we are leading lives that reflect our thoughts that are full of fears, obsessions, hate, jealousy, and again the list goes on. James 1:17 said, "Every good and perfect gift is from above, and cometh down from the Father of lights, with whom is no variableness, neither shadow of turning."

It's a gift to have a healthy mind-set. It affects your whole body and life and the people around you. Don't you agree to have a healthy, prosperous thought pattern is indeed a gift from God? Now don't get confused. A healthy mind-set is given to you because you have the power to keep it healthy and throw out the junk that pollutes your heart, mind, and life. God says that whatever we set our hands and hearts to do, He will prosper us while doing whatever we set out to do. He also says that whatever we choose to do, He will bless us as long as it's lovely, just, pure, and lines up to His Word.

Many people, not just atheists, overthink. How does God know everything? And if He knows everything, then in their head, they believe it makes Him responsible for our good or bad day-to-day choices. Just because God knows everything, it does not make Him responsible for what we choose to do in our day-to-day basis. How does one's knowing transfer to one's doing? It doesn't! The awesome thing about God knowing everything is that when we meditate and ask Him things and seek Him in the high places or high frequencies is that He guides our paths—all of them, the mental paths—that create our reality. He guides us into righteousness. He is our Shepherd, and goodness, I love Him!

I'm pointing this out using both terminology of God's written Word and modern science and both came from God. Let me clarify that all wisdom, knowledge, understanding, power, new discoveries, and groundbreaking research that really aren't so new in God's eyes, they all came from God giving us these enlightenments that have shaped our world, humanity, and creation today. God says there is no new thing done under the sun. It may be new to us, but to Him, He has already seen it. Remember, in order for God to know something, He must have already seen it all once before.

2

Trending Sin and Self-Power to Accomplish What He Commands

He is called the God of the past that existed even to the point where we may not even have proof of. I mean, do you really think that this book, the Bible, covers every single thing of God? It doesn't. You can't exhaust God! John 21:25 said, "Jesus did many other things as well. If every one of them were written down, I suppose that even the whole world would not have room for the books that would be written."

He gave mankind what He knew would be just enough to know Him and search Him out for ourselves in relationship with Him. I have my own lingo with God as do you! I have two daughters, and the way they have relationship to me or to their dad are entirely different from each other! He is the God of the present that is existing and the God of the future, that He already fixed. He seen the future that existed, that would leave us as humanity without Himself, without Godly power that trumps any demonic power in our world today, allowing for the godly to succeed as mankind having dominance, preeminence, and supreme authority over wicked governments in our physical day and our spiritual.

Evil can advance as much as they would like, but God already foresaw their success in wickedness, being the God that knows everything. He has created an escape route and upper hand, the enemy to be our footstool, and a launching pad, an evil that the enemy meant for harm to be turned around for God's glory, success, and triumph.

See when we win, God wins, and when He wins, we win on all levels in all categories—spiritually, mentally, physically, and nationally.

God is always speaking of us in a battle and in a battle for what? Battle for godly influence to reign because evil influence is trying to dominate with all kinds of perversion. They don't even call it evil anymore with homosexuality and their being countless numbers of so-called genders. When in fact demons are influencing their minds and hearts. Wiles of the enemy, he looks for those that are devourable like a roaring lion. Murder has become a trend with that. Abortion is one of the highest evils. From conception to birth, they disguise murder with the term *abortion*.

Individuals care more about a dog being euthanized or a murderer being euthanized. Individuals seem to have a problem with killing these two types of things but see it as "health care" when it comes to killing their own baby in their womb or outside of their womb. People fight so hard for the choice to simply kill a baby but fight for an animal to live and could care less if the murderer lives. They rather keep criminals and murderers alive by funding all their expenses for food, shelter, health care, entertainment, and education! I salute and applaud the Trump administration for bringing back the death penalty for federal crimes! I'm still applauding President Donald J. Trump for all of the success he continues to bring to America! I am honored and proud that I was born and raised in the United States of America that will resume capital punishments. Thank you, Attorney General William Barr. Thank you, Department of Justice!

Don't you know that God utterly destroyed and destroys His enemies! He wanted King Agag killed. In 1 Samuel 15:18, it said, "And the Lord sent you on a mission, and said, 'Go, totally destroy the sinners, the Amalekites and fight against them until they are eliminated.'" King Agag was a notorious serial killer along with his wicked or brainwashed nation that had continuously used guerrilla warfare to attack Israel. It said in 1 Samuel 15:32, "Then Samuel said, 'Bring me Agag, the king of the Amalekites.'" And Agag came to him delicately, cheerfully, and in chains.

Haven't you seen these ridiculous criminals on TV that scoff and brag about their crimes and disrespect the prison officers? That is what Agag was appearing like when brought to Samuel. And Agag said, "Surely, the bitterness of death has come to an end."

Samuel said, "As your sword has made women childless, so shall your mother be childless among women." And Samuel cut Agag in pieces before the Lord in Gilgal. People need to understand that God is not a human. He made humans! He is the first and the last and the beginning and the end. He didn't just write the law and decrees; He is it! He is vengeance itself! He truly can say He made us and can take us out of this world. We truly are an open book to God. He knows every single day laid out. He knows our outcome and what kind of person we will be.

In the following scriptures, many are torn on how God commands that even infants, mothers, and children are to be slaughtered that are Amalekites. Galatians 6:7–8, "Be not deceived God is not mocked: for whatsoever a man soweth that shall he also reap. For he that soweth to his flesh shall of the flesh reap corruption; but he that soweth to the Spirit shall of the Spirit reap life everlasting." This decree of complete annihilation over the Amalekites was their due judgement summoned by Agag himself, he reaped what he sowed many times over. When he had his people the Amalekites ambush and kill the women, children and men of Israel for no reason he was going to reap the consequences for that, especially when brutally attacking the Children of God. Just like Job, Jobs paranoia caused his family to perish. His worst fears came upon him. It was Jobs constant fear that summoned Satan to the courts of God and gave full permission to his worst nightmares to unfold in his life. Simply put God only decreed the judgement that Agag sentenced his clan and himself too when he sowed death to the Israelites. He destined himself and his clan to complete annihilation. The pharaoh, when he sowed death to all the firstborn of Israel, he also sowed death to his own first born and all of Egypt's firstborn. God is The Righteous Judge that will only decree what people have sown to themselves! When Agag harmed God's Children he summoned full annihilation to his own bloodline!

God is righteous forever! Amen! Countless scriptures declare that God is an all-knowing God. So If God declared that all be completely destroyed, then He knows thoroughly—complete with regard to every detail, not superficial or partial. He had to guide the Israelites to safety for themselves and their children and generations to come. Today we have laws, governments, and kingdoms in place that can protect us and our generations that will follow! Israel did not have these structures of laws and kingdoms and dominions in place. They were still evolving into a nation and a country. So, yes, it was a crucial decree that was necessary to advance and keep Israel alive.

Imagine you being a family of two hundred family members against a whole tribe or group of family that are of three hundred people, and they are a vicious notorious, ruthless, dangerous, and psychotic group or clan or familia. It truly is to kill or be killed, or your children will endure their offspring to be jeopardized and slaughtered as well. This is a decree that is not for our day and era. We have evolved and have weapons and rescue teams in place that can deal with taking out the bad and saving the children and mothers so as long as they're not a terrorist or radicalized at a young age to kill our children.

Please understand that God is not stupid, my goodness. He made you and everything else.

> Thus says the Lord of Hosts and Armies, "I will punish the Amalekites for what they did to Israel when they waylaid them as they came up from Egypt. Now go and attack the Amalekites and completely destroy everything that they have; do not spare them, put to death men and women, children & infants, cattle and sheep, camels and donkeys." (1 Samuel 15:2–3)

Did God show mercy to the Pharaoh? Did God punish David for brutally beheading Goliath? He used Cain in the beginning to show others the penalty for murdering. However, did that punishment cause people to obey? No!! There are countless scriptures of God being a blameless righteous judge.

> And the Heavens declare his righteousness, for God himself is Judge. Selah. (Psalms 50:6)

> As for God, his way is perfect: the way of the Lord is tried: He is a buckler to all those that trust in Him! (Psalms 18:30)

See, God being a perfect, flawless, and blameless judge had to cover all His bases and deal with all of this thoroughly. He didn't just kill Cain who committed the first murder without using him as an example to prevent murder from continuously happening. However, that standard or consequence did not prevent people from committing such evil acts. God shows Himself blameless to mankind. He allows evolving to take place. He won't just jump to the evolved state that we will be fifty years down the road. He works with us. He builds us and creates character and endurance within us and our genetics. So, no, we do not follow that failed consequence that was demonstrated through Cain. So God gave us and shaped us into evolved governments, laws of the lands, kingdoms, and dominions allowing official decrees that shape and hold our nations and make us fortified countries around the world today.

The death penalty is a fair warning stating the very clear penalty for such heinous acts! God sees it as pure disobedience, cowardliness, and laziness to not deal with the children of Satan! They know God's righteous decree that those that do such things deserve death (Romans 1:32)! Jesus says in Matthew 18:6, Mark 9:42, and Luke 17:2, "Kill these wastes of life! And whosoever shall offend one of these little ones that believe in Me, it is better for him that a millstone were hung around his neck and he were cast into the sea!" Criminals should be put to death, says Jesus three times!

Milestones weigh 3,300 pounds! Do not be like King Saul who kept the criminal alive! Understand that God is for destroying evil demonic people, and He defends the righteous, yes, with vengeance toward their enemies!! Balance, people. You must balance!! It's crucial to become mature in these things! We must know when certain things apply!! God does not contradict Himself! He wants us to use wisdom in everything! God showed mercy to Saul of Tarsus because Saul was passionate with wrong zeal for God.

Like many Jews today, they do not believe in Jesus the Messiah. They strictly believe only in God Yahweh! Saul was a devout Jew, and God knew Saul's zeal for the Lord God and seen Jesus as a confusion and was faithful to his God by trying to end the idea of Jesus! Well, God knew that Saul needed understanding because Saul really loved God Yahweh and was trying to stand up for God! Well, Jesus seen this and so did God, and they said to themselves, "Saul, with understanding that Jesus truly is the Messiah and backed by God, will inform the world of the truth about Jesus."

Saul was incredibly passionate and did just that. He wrote most of all the New Testament! Saul was not depraved in his mind, so, no, do not throw him into the category of notorious serial killer and think that we should be merciful to depraved individuals! Later, Saul was given a new name that became Paul the apostle. God commanded Samuel, David, Joshua, and many more people to kill evil individuals. He commanded Simon and Peter to not draw the sword because the high priest's servant, Malchus, was not a vicious evil serial killer and that there was no need to strike him. God commanded the law of the land to be abided.

So the one governing sets those laws and punishments in place and those that resist will bring judgment on themselves (Romans 13:1–2)! If they choose to kill anyone or molest a child, they choose the death penalty! Christians are concerned with notorious serial killers finding Jesus when that individual should have found Jesus prior to brutally molesting, dismembering, and murdering infants, children, women, elderly, and innocent men!!! Christians, stop separating Old Testament and New Testament like one is not God! No! God wants us to balance, rule, judge! Not sit like scared kitty cats!! Proverbs 11:1 states, "A false balance is an abomination to the Lord and dishonest scales the Lord detests. But accurate weight finds favor with Him, just weight is His delight!"

Self-Power Is the Great I Am

These two major topics are some of the successful surfacing wickedness in our world today, more successful than ever. There are many more agendas that are still in the making to become a so-called trend, breakthrough, what they call love and equal opportunity is. Here's one phrase—"love has no limits." Sounds great, right? But they are using this in a perverse manner. Evil understands that all humanity is a creation that creates, and in order for us to create, we evolve. So mixing evil and good together becomes a very difficult idea or thing to separate. It takes godly wisdom to apply love and truth to set the captives free. God allows the wickedness to run rampant and become loud because then He makes them look ridiculous allowing common sense to beam through them like a laughingstock that they are. Satan works with half-truths to create a perfect, effective lie that is impossible for some to see if they are not filled with God.

I am not here to walk on tippy-toes. I am here to shine light on rapid progressing stupidity or sins that are spreading like wildfire due to perversion all over the world today. I am not here to walk on tippy-toes. I speak the truth that many are so afraid to stand for. The reason why corrupt people today demand Christianity to agree that their sin and lifestyle including homosexuality and all kinds of immoral living and perversion be accepted by God, Jesus, Holy Spirit, and Christians today is because they know that we are the supreme authority. And without our say, they still are wrong, incorrect, lawless, dishonorable, untrue, false, off target, corrupt, confused, and mistaken. They seek our permission as Christians and don't even know it.

The world wants us to condone to their filthy ways and evil ways because they know we hold the power to say that they're wrong, and if we say that they're right, then they feel free. They want us to confess that there is no evil when really, all knees will bend and every tongue will confess Jesus Christ as Lord because it's true. See, God can make that knee of yours bend and make your mouth confess your maker only because He is the truth and you will show respect in the presence of God. If demons tremble at His name, you better believe that knee will hit the ground and that tongue will confess the truth even when you want to deny it, but it's impossible to confess a lie in the presence of God when you know what is the truth and God would never make you confess a lie or kneel at a false God. Yes, atheists will kneel and confess the same for Satanist and all that are sinners. Even if they don't want to kneel or confess, that will be something that He will make the individuals do (Philippians 2:10–11; Romans 14:11; Revelations 5:13)!

See, God was the first one to declare that it's immoral and that these certain ways of living were wrong and lawless and corrupt so that's why wicked people have a problem with us. The fact that they are trying again to fight for their corrupt ways on all levels of corruption is because God silenced them a long time ago, and now, they're trying to surface their corrupt ways again. I'm here to say that evil is evil and just because people have continued to brainwash humanity with men liking men and women liking women and men trying to be women and women trying to be men. I'm here to declare that their corrupt is evil. It's confusion, and yes, it's dishonorable to God in the highest level. Yes, it's an abomination.

When you deny who you are and deny what kind of human you're made for, you burn up nations within you. Do you know that a small fetus or baby girl in the womb has already as many eggs in her tiny womb that could populate forty small countries estimating at seven million eggs? For a female to be with a woman, she will never have children the way that her creator made her to have children. And for lesbians to adopt, they are teaching that little child confusion and corruption. For a man to be with a man, that sperm will go nowhere to become a human. It will constantly be wasted and never multiply and again. For homosexuals to adopt or have a surrogate, you have destined that child with confusion and corruption. Just because they want to not change and give the constant excuse that they can't change, they destine others to become lawless and confused. It's wrong. It's evil, and that is why God has the truth. So when a confused individual identifies that they are believing a lie, then they can become free.

Sodom and Gomorrah burnt up because, yes, of the clear perversion but also an example that they would eventually kill themselves off because man was not with woman, and if there had been a

Self-Power Is the Great I Am

man with a woman and that woman conceived and actually was able to have a child, that child would have ended up molested and most likely be killed. Keep in mind the men there wanted to have sex with angels! God is right forever and ever!!! Woah to those that call good evil and evil good and blessed are those who are not offended!

Christians must be blatant about what sin is yet not unloving! God is love, but He hates what He hates and wants us to hate what He hates and love what He loves. We absolutely hate the sin and love the sinner. We must have clear answers for our loved ones that are in confusion. Because ultimately, God is the righteous Judge, and He will judge their hearts. Our instruction is to gently encourage the sinner away from evil and to be careful not to agree with their sin. We're allowing them to perish if we say nothing. We must warn them and have ready answers.

This world wants to change the laws for evil behavior, but reality check, you can't change the kingdom of God's law in His own kingdom. He says what is permitted there and murderers that love to murder aren't all abortionist! And neither are homosexuals if they want to stay in their lawlessness. Liars that love to lie and people full of hate that love to hate are not permitted. Man and woman full of lust that love to sleep around are not permitted either. They practice no self-control a.k.a. *self-power*!!!

Get mad. I don't care! I'm not the God who made us and the one who set instructions for mankind; God is. I love people enough to tell them the truth. Wounds from a sincere friend are better than many kisses from an enemy! God's vengeance is scarier than hell itself. God was the one who made hell and the one who casted out Satan or Lucifer from the heavens with the third of heaven along with him. God wiped out nations with floods, fires, and the earth swallowing them. You really think He cares about the evil people that are trying to brainwash mankind with their stupidity? People must understand God is love, but *He* doesn't love sin and people that want to stay in their sin!! He says over and over that He clearly will pit Himself against them. New Testament is all about having the grace to do all that God commanded us to do with the law in the Old Testament (Matthew 5:17–18). How evildoers wish that New Testament permitted them to sin. Shameful! You have another thing coming and that is why He calls fools, fools!!

Homosexuality used to have a phrase tied to it that went like this, "Coming out of the closet." Repeat those words, "Coming out of the closet." Someone must have been hiding in a closet. Why? When someone hides in a closet, they are hiding from something scary or dangerous. Something that is causing them to be afraid. It's terrifying to lose who you are. Confusion in any category of life is burdensome and frightening. A decision that cannot land because of uncertainty is obviously confusion. God is the author of truth and peace. Satan is the father of confusion and fear. He is a grand manipulator, and he is a forceful ruler. God is a gentleman. God would never cause confusion on anyone of His precious creations. So if one has become confused, fearful, shamed, perverse, even since childhood, they have been tricked and lied to. Somewhere they have been enticed to such an idea—yes, even as a child, even more so as a child.

Generational curses are prior genes affecting the next offspring. What your ancestors struggled with or where they were exposed to evil will have an effect on you. That's why the scripture says we were born into sin, and that's why we must become a new creation in Christ Jesus, abandoning the lies that we have let identify us and breaking out of the embodiment of trickery.

I have counseled homosexuals who cry for they feel broken, and it has always been my heart to have answers of truth that can help them heal and be set free. They have fallen in love with the captor of deceit. There are countless cases where an abused victim falls in love with their abuser because they have been shown love or so-called love during their abuse. Homosexuality is influenced by a deceiving spirit especially if there was ever exposure to an individual through rape or abuse or pornography or even in the bloodline that has imprinted on the individuals genetics.

Science proves that how we think, we are in fact creating our body to respond to it genetically. God says that as we think, so are we. But this does not always mean that were thinking and choosing to believe righteousness.

Self-Power Is the Great I Am

Galatians 6:3 (NIV) states, "If anyone thinks they are something when they are not, they deceive themselves." Homosexuals, transgenders, and every confused individual that thinks they are something else than what they are are only tricking themselves. Believe me, their brain believes it. Science proves that our brains do not distinguish from what's real or not. That's why we must know what is a lie from Satan and untrue from the father of lies, and we must know what is the truth and from God the one that can't lie. God doesn't want us to be deceived by false truths because He knows we can believe it and become whatever we imagine, just like science once again has proved God is right again.

Whatsoever you believe, you shall receive, and how a person thinks, so are they. That's why you can see evil people doing such horrific things to other people such as abortion—murder in the womb and murder all over the world, perversion toward our innocent children in the world—and now trying to brainwash our young into homosexuality! Get away, you evildoers! Men and women, rise up and shame the wicked!

When we shower love, which is good and godly toward a confused hurting individual, and then do a wicked thing and continue to tell them that the thing that is causing them to fear is actually good for them. We have created a very wicked blend of truths and lies that they can't separate. The enemy being a forceful evil that he is leads confused individuals that are like sheep led straight to the slaughter. The enemy comes to steal, kill, and destroy, and God comes to give life and life more abundantly. God loves the homosexual, that is why He gave His life for every sinner. We have all fallen short of the glory of God because we have been born into sin or a blood of genetics that have been destined with corruption. Homosexuals are drinking from the cup of poison, and Christians sit there with no answers to save them! Shame on Christians for not having the boldness of love to gently correct them and to powerfully encourage them.

Leviticus 18:22, Leviticus 20:13 along with 1 Corinthians 5 are condemning same-sex sexual relations. Romans 1:31 states, "Without understanding, covenant breakers, without natural affection, implacable, their senseless, faithless, heartless and unmerciful."

This is also condemning pedophilia and rape. It's a sin, and God will pit Himself against any individual who takes advantage of a child in any form of sexual assault or abuse.

Matthew 18:5–6 states, "And anyone who welcomes a little child like this on my behalf is welcoming me. But if someone causes one of these little ones who trusts in me to fall into sin such as molesting them and causing them to be hurt physically and confused mentally as they grow up, such as being confused whether they are a man or a woman." God says it would be better for someone to ring their neck with a chain and tie their inhumane disgusting, sick, evil, demonic self to a massive milestone and carelessly toss this trash into the sea to be drowned as they scream for their lives! Matthew 18:7 states, "Woe to the world and what sorrow awaits the world because it tempts people to sin and causes them to stumble." Temptations are inevitable, but what sorrow awaits the person who does the tempting. What God will do to the person that molested a child is unimaginable revenge!

> Vengeance is mine, and recompense; Their foot shall slip in due time; For the day of their calamity is at hand, and the things to come hasten upon them! (Deuteronomy 32:35)

> Do not be afraid and fear the one who can kill your body but the one who can kill the soul; rather fear Him who is able to destroy both your body and your soul in hell! (Matthew 10:28)

God calls wicked lawless people *inventors of sin*!! *They invent new sick ways to sin!*

Since they thought it's foolish to acknowledge God, He left them or abandoned them to their foolish thinking and *let them do things that should never be done* (Romans 1:28)! Their lives became full of every kind of wickedness, sin, greed, hate, envy, murder, quarreling, deception, malicious behavior, and gossip. They are backstabbers and haters of God—insolent, proud, and boastful. *They invent new ways of sinning,* and they disobey their parents. They refuse to understand because they don't want to understand. They don't want to listen or change. They hate good. They hate things of God! They break their promises, are heartless, and have no mercy. They know God's justice requires that those who do these things *deserve to die*!! Yet they do them anyway! Worse yet, they encourage others to do them too!

But God shows His anger from heaven against all sinful, wicked people who suppress the truth by their wickedness (Romans 1:18). They know the truth about God because He has made it obvious to them. For ever since the world was created, people have seen the earth and sky, and now we have discovered outer space and the galaxies. Unbelievers have no excuse. Atheists have no excuse to not believe that there is a creator—the one and only true God! How about they beg us to prove to them they have a brain in their skull? Or that we need oxygen to breathe? Or our earth has a sun and moon? Through everything God made, they can clearly see His invisible qualities—His eternal power and divine nature. So they have no excuse for not knowing God!

Yes, they knew God, but they wouldn't worship Him as God or even give Him thanks (Romans 1:21). And they began to think up foolish ideas of what God was like. As a result, their minds became dark and confused. Science and the medical field show that brain scans of criminals, serial killers, and depressed individuals are dark compared to a healthy brain scan. Claiming to be wise, they instead became utter fools. And instead of worshiping the glorious, ever-living God, they worshiped idols made to look like mere people, animals, birds, and reptiles.

Molech, the false man-made god of their time, required homosexual sex to be an offering and required babies to be burned alive. Trending sin today is abortion and homosexuality along with LGBTQ confusion! Yes, I said it, and I'll say it again—it's confusion. In my personal opinion, it's garbage. By the time they're done completing their group's title, it will look like the alphabet! You know why they can't stop adding another category of sexual preferences to their group title? Because confusion can't ever rest. People that are in confusion do not rest. Anyone can call me homophobic, and I'll call you confused (Deuteronomy 4:28; Psalms 115:4; Romans 1:24). So God abandoned them to do whatever shameful things their hearts desired. As a result, they did vile and degrading things with each other's bodies. They traded the truth about God for a lie. So they worshiped and served the things God created instead of the creator Himself who is worthy of eternal praise! Amen. That is why God abandoned them to their shameful desires. Even the women turned against the natural way to have sex and instead indulged in sex with each other. And the men, instead of having normal sexual relations with women, burned with lust for each other. Men did shameful things with other men, and as a result of this sin, they suffered within themselves—the penalty they deserved such as *diseases, obviously. LGBTQ commercials have paid ads on protecting yourselves if you're having same-sex sexual relations. Disgusting and against God in the highest.*

However, when the homosexual has fallen in love with their intoxicating sin and doesn't want to change, they have created a reality that is against God. Just because you have mixed some good with evil and live comfortable in your disobedience and bondage, it doesn't make you right. It's perverse, end of story. Man should not be with man. Woman should not be with woman. Family should not be with family or human to their animals, adults with children. It's evil, and it's wrong, and if Christians can't identify what is evil and cunning and Satan is disguised as this big Valentine present, then we are not going to preserve mankind. Man should not wear women's clothing, and women should not wear men's clothing (Deuteronomy 22:5). In our modern day, this is known as drag queen or cross-dressing. Yet the world wants to encourage children to be a cross-dresser! Deuteronomy 27 and all of Deuteronomy and, my goodness, Exodus and some of Genesis goes on and on about these sins.

We are called to be the salt of the earth. We are to help our brothers and sisters when they have been lied to and been manipulated into believing that sin is good and there is no evil. Truth will set you free and lies will tell you that the addiction won't kill you. Can we say to the liar that lying is impossible to change? Can we say to the abuser that abusing others is impossible to change? Can we say to the murderer that murder is impossible to change? Can we say to the rapist that raping is impossible to change? Can we say to the pedophile that pedophilia is impossible to change? Can we say to the drug addict that drug addiction is impossible to change? Can we say to the sex addict and prostitutes that sex addiction and prostitution is impossible to change? Can we say to the thief that stealing is impossible to change? Why then should we say that homosexuality is impossible to change?

"I tried and I can't change"—this phrase should then be applied to all impossibilities of sin. Then we should believe that with all sin across the board that all sin is impossible to change. It's so comical that people throughout time have acted like what God asks and commands of us to do is so outrageous and overbearing. Do you or does anyone like when a close friend or family member lies to them? Or a spouse cheats on them? No, you don't. Well, God was the one who gave us this rule, including everything else that makes sense! People that want their stupid and vile ways are the ones that complain! Well, I love the ways of the Lord! *Impossible* is actually written with two words—*I'm* and *possible*. Say to yourself, "The things that I consider are impossible in my life are actually possible because I'm possible to change anything that is against God!" Seriously, everyone wants to be around people that are moral, decent, vivacious, cheerful, vigorous, confident, strong, brave, tough, resilient, wise, funny, etc.! So stop acting or pretending like God's commands are stupid when people are the ones who are stubborn and stupid!

See the sinner themselves must humble themselves, not in guiltiness, not in shame, but with brokenness in their heart to say, "I'm not perfect, Lord, but I know that You can't lie. That You made me and You call me holy like You, and I can and will be made holy like You. I hate what You hate. I love what You love, and I say wash me clean, make me brand-new. Lord Jesus, You died for my sin and made me brand-new! Transform me, Lord! Cause me to be repulsed with the sin that I have drunk so deeply of. Cause all my wicked friends and associates to want nothing to do with me, drive them all away! I forgive myself for my sin because the old person was never me. I am called the righteousness of God and that is me!"

The sinner must say, "Jesus, come into my heart. I need You to be the supreme authority! I will make my confusion disappear by meditating on Your truth. I will listen to the truth. I will heal and use my God-given self-power for the things that will make me brand-new and glorify You, Lord."

This next topic was not something that I was going to teach. I was going to save this for volume 2 of my book. I kept thinking that I was done with my book, and God kept talking in my heart. So here it is. If a sinner remains a sinner and blasphemous or does not change from their wickedness and dies in their sin, the love and mercy of God will still meet them in the spiritual realm to show them that He is the great I am. Hoping that they will turn from their evil, God knowing their hearts crystal clear and far better than themselves will be the supreme Judge on if they are fit for the kingdom of God or not.

Put it this way: He will know if their authentic in humility or putting up a front to just lie and remain corrupt. Many unsaved individuals in our time and era have had near-death experiences and have encountered God and made amends. Some cases where they are pronounced dead and brought back to life somehow have spoken of a God encounter. Luke 16 specifies about a certain rich man. This rich man ended up in hell, and the story is that he is not received into Abraham's bosom or paradise. He's not in hell because he was rich. He was in hell because of a wicked heart that God knew would never change. Just because we see him begging doesn't mean he is changing in his heart. He is only in it for himself so that he is taken care of. King Solomon was incredibly wealthier than him, and well, many people in the Bible were wealthy beyond belief! My point here is that you see the stories written in Luke 15 and 16 are famous ones—the lost sheep that God will leave the ninety-nine for the one.

Next story is the prodigal son. Romans 8:31–39 is regarding the *powerful relentless love of God*! How nothing can separate us, not any angels or demons, not hell or heaven, and not our fears or worries for today or tomorrow can separate us from God's love. Stay with me when I'm delivering something that will help you if you have ever been concerned about a loved one not receiving Jesus or one that passed and never knew God on earth.

God will heal the homosexual and the sinner even if they happen to die on earth and die in their sin. Stay with me if they change their minds and confess Jesus as Lord and Savior—yes, in the spiritual realm—and if God will leave the ninety-nine living on earth and chase the one lost one in death to show His grand love to them because earthly realms and spiritual realms don't separate us from God's love. I'm certain that when they see how His love for them has caused Him to chase them down through the realms, I imagine that they are brought to tears and humility. I'm confident that God will transform them in a moment if they wish to be healed and pleasing to God.

Sure, they have their God-given self-power to change and heal in this moment right now but many people *choose to overthink*. A true return of the prodigal child returning to the Father! Even in hell, the psalmist cries God is there! If a sinner gets saved in the earthly realm, they can be saved in the spiritual realm (Psalm 139:8). In God's presence, if they have a true heart for change even in the spirit, there are some people that granted they have such a desire to change; however, were stuck or are stuck or overthinking and hindering themselves to not change their old ways and are hindering themselves in operating in their self-power to heal by believing what God said. But they have a genuine heart to change and find it very difficult and feel like they are not worthy and love God. God sees that heart that they want to change and don't' know how. This heart is humble. But don't think you can deceive Him either.

God says that He will help us in our unbelief; however, I promise you this, God knows the difference between an individual that is authentic and genuine to want to change but allows confusion in without knowing. Or if the individual is a liar and wicked and thinks he can trick or fool God. I want to make clear that I'm not condoning wickedness and sin by telling you that you will have one more chance to receive Jesus if you accidentally die or if you choose to deliberately sin until death and think like magic words that you can say, "I'm sorry, God. I really love you now."

Jybe Yvves

Not all who say, "Lord, Lord," will enter His kingdom. God knows your heart. He is the Father of hearts and all spirits. He knows our innermost thoughts and will do away with wicked individuals like the man in Luke in the spiritual realm that was in hades talking to Abraham. Jesus went to hell and the grave just for us. He became our sin when He knew none. He already went from earth realm to spiritual realm for us, showing us that His love, power, and might are never separated from us unless after all of that one refuses Him still.

Three years ago in Visalia, California, I woke up at 4 a.m. with a racing heart and a bit frightened due to a very surreal dream. In the dream, it's nighttime at the ocean. It's very windy and the powerful ocean waves are crashing and the shoreline is continuing to rise. I, however, was on the shoreline on solid ground, and I noticed this woman was frantically digging two graves on the dangerous shorelines. I was concerned for her and was shouting to her. I eventually went to her, and as she turned, she looked normal and then appeared in her face with red-and-white paint and became distorted and demonic looking.

I began to grab her by the arms and pray very powerfully in the Holy Spirit or in tongues. I have prayed in the Holy Ghost for twelve years now. Anyways, as I prayed, she remained demonic and unchanging. I woke up and wanted to know what the dream had meant. Well, God gave clear answers. He said there are people out there that won't change even if they were shown the power of God. They love their sin and will continue to dig their own graves. Even unto death and even in the spiritual realm, they love their wickedness and won't change. Even if God Himself shows them in the clearest form of His love to them.

We, as the body of Christ, need to have a backbone and realize evil is evil. God made clear to me that she had no power over me while praying in the Holy Spirit but also made it clear that we can't change those that want to remain evil and teach evil. The oceans represented that God was letting her dig her own graves, and yes, He was, in fact, letting the ocean drown her just like in the days of Noah. Understand that wicked people and evil things will never be accepted by God!

Self-Power Is the Great I Am

Wake up, church!!!!! Be an angry father of righteousness and an angry mother of righteousness! Whether you're actually a mother or father, have that spirit, that heart and mind of one! Stop being afraid of what corrupted and confused people will think of you! My goodness, be full of righteous anger! Tear down the principalities of evil. Be fearless! Who cares if you lose popularity or lose friends and family! Jesus said, "I came to bring a sword, not peace!" He came to bring peace for godliness and a sword to evil.

> Do not suppose that I have come to bring peace to the earth. I did not come to bring peace, but a sword. For I have come to turn "a man against his father, a daughter against her mother, a daughter-in-law against her mother-in-law—a man's enemies will be the members of his own household." (Matthew 10:34–36)

Meaning, that friends including family most likely will hate you or be offended with you.

> Anyone who loves their father or mother more than me is not worthy of me. Whoever does not take up their own cross and follow me is not worthy of me! Whoever finds their life will lose it, and whoever loses their life for my sake will find it. (Matthew 10:37–39)

In Matthew 10, Jesus called His twelve disciples and gave them much instruction.

> I am sending you out like sheep among wolves. Therefore be as shrewd as snakes and as innocent as doves. Be on your guard; you will be handed over to the local councils and be flogged in the synagogues. On my account, you will be brought before governors and kings as witnesses to them

> and the Gentiles. But when they arrest you, do not worry about what to say or how to say it. At that time, you will be given what to say for it will not be you speaking but the Spirit of your Father speaking through you. (Matthew 10:16–20)

This again is the entwinement of God and us being absolutely one and proving again our self-power.

> Brother will betray brother to death, and a father his child; children will rebel against their parents and have them put to death. You will be hated by everyone because of me, but the one who stands firm to the end will be saved. When you are persecuted in one place, flee to another! Truly I tell you, you will not finish going through the towns of Israel before the son of man comes. (Matthew 10:21–23)

He is clearly telling us that we must all speak up or we're not worthy of even uttering His name. We're all a bunch of chickens!

Here's to the unbeliever, and here's to the stagnant and unproductive Christian. He is the first and the last. No one created God. You expect that because we understand how something comes from something, but don't you understand that that system comes from the one who is, was, and is to come? There was no God before Him or beside Him. He shows us the future and helps us in every way. He actually navigates us through time and our lives to live out His best plan for us so we can prosper and our children and lineage can prosper in all areas! In order for God to know everything, He must have seen it all before. Hebrews 11:3 states, "Through faith we understand that the worlds, universes, and ages were framed by the word of God, so that things which are seen were not made of things which do appear."

Before the foundations of the earth, before He spoke one word to create even one of us, before there was one bacteria or oxygen or gravity, before it all—*He imagined* or *imaged* us and creation and everyone's scenarios and beliefs and fears and every single thought

Self-Power Is the Great I Am

from every single individual. He knew before He opened His mouth to create us. He had seen how we would fall, and then He created a way to fix it, to cause a cure or an antibiotic if you will to save us as humanity. He had seen the power in humanity that would come from Himself that with the blessing of free will that He formed us with would be dangerous to humanity so He allowed us to have Jesus, self-power, truth, and confidence in knowing as His true sons and daughters, all of mankind, that could bring enlightenment to the rest of the broken world even the brokenness in professing Christians.

The kingdom of God suffers violence and the violent take it by force. It's talking about obviously one group of mankind that is of evil that is causing the kingdom of God to suffer and another group of humanity that is of God that is actually good. The group of humanity that is for godliness is more passionate and full of violence toward the demonic realm that needs to get back in submission. God is trying to get mankind on a higher frequency, the frequency of pure power and relationship with Him, what was once known as the "walking in the cool of the day with God" before the *fall or lower frequency we were once on or our genetics were once on.*

To conclude here, yes, all of our days are laid before Him like an open book, and He knows every scenario of each decision we will think and possibly choose and I'm thankful for it because He helps me as I live my life. Aren't you thankful that you have a guide and a God who knows it all? So you can cheat in life? Cheat in a good way. You don't have to do a trial and error, trial and error over and over. He has preserved His written Word for us so we can follow with basic powerful truths, and He has given us His Holy Spirit to be the great helper alongside! Your Google navigation knows each move you make and your destination. Even if you go outside the directions, it will reroute you, but it won't make you do anything you don't want to do. Same with your smartphones, it will begin to suggest things for you that you have been searching or talking and texting about.

Thought I'd leave you with a little extra example; however, God is on a much grander scale. No one or nothing can top Him. Don't cry about it. You're not God, and you never will be. Understand that He is the first Creator of atom, and we are the little branches creators that are incredible, phenomenal, and powerful just like Him because we are made in His image!

During meditation, make sure that what you create lines up to His written Word because He is a just God and He won't be mocked. Understand that we didn't make ourselves, that we are blessed with life, and that we do die and we have an afterlife. Understand that if your excuse is you can't change, then you're being lazy. Please don't take offense to my words if you are a person that is done with excuses; however, if you're an individual that fits the description of these next sentences, I hope it wakes you up out of your foolishness! Wounds from a sincere friend are better than many kisses from an enemy. You have chosen to not take responsibility to do your absolute best to become more like Him. Why should I become more like Him? You sound like a five-year-old saying, "I don't want to listen to my father or mother because I know what's best for myself." You demand of so many answers that you do nothing with when given the truth and wisdom that will set you free! You rather sit there looking the same, dealing with your own pollution that you don't want to take responsibility for or change it! Though you are so quick to blame God for it, how about changing your perspective and doing the very best to change to heal to prosper to become more like Him!

We were all born into sin or rather missing the mark… A better definition of sin is missing the frequency of life that we were destined to have that would have held us in life and through humanity. We have the fall of man to blame for that. What does that word *fall* mean? Fall from what? That is a unique word to use to describe the thing that separates us from God. If there was a "fall," their must have been somewhere higher that we as mankind fell from. The first man and woman that God chose to work through had our combination of genetics that were of a high calling or frequency or radio wave that our genetics once were from. When man and woman disobeyed and caused trickery, confusion, and distrust toward God, they ruined the frequency for the genetics or the lineage of all mankind. To be perfectly union with God or to have clear reception or perfect connection with the creator is now put back together with our will through Jesus and self-power.

3
God Created Meditation and Self-Power for the Believer

The world practices these gifts apart from God. Science is God waking up His sleeping body. Neuroscience states that we have over fifty thousand to seventy thousand thoughts a day. No wonder God calls us kings. Fifty thousand to seventy thousand thoughts are a tremendous number for one person to manage or rule over. You must be given some divine power or more like self-power to manage all those unseen things all by yourself. If you are an undisciplined queen or king over your mind, you are in shambles!

In 2 Corinthians 10:3–5, it declares, "For though we walk in the flesh, we are not waging war according to the flesh." We use God's mighty weapons, not tangible weapons from this world. Our weapons have divine power, says the Lord. Again, it is self-power to demolish the strongholds also known as the patterns of thinking of human reasoning and to destroy false arguments. We obliterate every proud obstacle, argument, and every pretension that sets itself up against the knowledge of God. We take captive every rebellious thought to make it obey Christ. In order to be a queen or king, you have to have self-power. If you don't operate in your self-power, you are a slave to the powerful machine that is running nonstop called your mind.

Famous neuroscientists today boast that they have figured a system out that can cause an individual to heal themselves and others along with other unlimited potential. In order to prove this method, neuroscientists monitor the brain frequencies as the individuals meditate. Neuroscientists teach that while meditating, one must focus on something greater than themselves. The people that are changing their thoughts are indeed changing themselves and ridding themselves of the old self. In order to purge mental illness or physical ailments and diseases, neuroscientists state that individuals must be releasing love and forgiveness. One must acknowledge a greater power within themselves. They say that the person must feel the emotion before changing their thinking that neurons that fire together, wire together. A new personality creates a new reality. Why must the individual be releasing love and forgiveness along with gratitude? Because they create new neurons to fire and wire, releasing chemical responses that allow the individual to feel and to eventually heal. If negative thoughts and feelings break down our bodies, then positive thoughts and feelings can heal our bodies.

Scripture states in Ephesians 4:14, "So that we may no longer be children, tossed to and fro by feelings and emotions and carried about by every wind or thought of doctrine, by human cunning, by craftiness in deceitful schemes." Remember, feelings are like waves and thoughts are like winds. They move you or cause you to have an emotion. Science has proven that words and thoughts change water molecules, even written words on pieces of paper change the makeup of even polluted water to a beautiful snowflake looking molecule of water. This study was done by Dr. Masaru Emoto. Please research and see how God's Word is being proven today.

We're 80 percent water, so what you're thinking creates your makeup and the makeup of your children. When a loved one gets sick, you can heal them because 80 percent of them is water, and you can speak to that water in their body to demonstrate healing, and it will! But if you doubt in your heart, you won't change anything. Thoughts are like winds; you can't see them. There are so many thoughts that are like strong winds or like tornadoes that can definitely cause you to be enlightened or confused. God is not the Father of confusion! Feeling is a great indication that the person is changing during meditation; however, the feelings must be positive feelings to reap the results. When the person is turning on frequencies, this is the lingo, meaning levels of deep state of meditation.

What makes my blood boil or causes a righteous anger in me is the fact that these teachings are all from God's written Word. And neuroscientists act like they came up with these principles and formulas all on their own. To do these deep meditations without God, you will still perish. You will not have eternal life without acknowledging God as your Lord and Savior, and don't you think that fact is a big hindrance while meditating? We must abide in God and Him in us. If your acknowledging the power in you without understanding who that power actually is, you will have half-truths. And even though one is experiencing miraculous things, they will still be missing so much more! People are amazed at the results with deep meditations such as the miracles, mystical, and somewhat magical effects there are with meditating; however, you can have all of this and still be missing 90 percent of the rest of the fullness of God.

Don't take God's wisdoms and act like you discovered something new. Give credit where it is due. Science is not the first one to utter these wisdoms; God is. And in fact, He says that all of wisdom, truth, common sense, and knowledge will heal all of your flesh and give you abundance of life and long life will you be satisfied with.

> My child do not forget my teaching, but let your heart keep my commandments; For length of days and life worth living And tranquility and prosperity the wholeness of life's blessings they will add to you. (Proverbs 3:1–2)

Okay, all of Proverbs is out of this world, outstanding, and puts any other book ever written to shame!

Here's another wonderful scripture telling you about God's words are healing your flesh. Science is not the first one to tell mankind the formulas of long and prosperous life. In fact, they take every command that God has given us and say it like they were the ones to discover it.

> My child pay attention to my words and be willing to learn; open your ears to my sayings. Do not let them escape from your sight; keep them in the center of your heart. For they are life to those who find them, And healing and health to all their flesh. Watch over your heart with all diligence, for from it flow the springs of life. (Proverbs 4: 20–23)

As you think, so are you! Jesus said it!! This is "groundbreaking science" called epigenetics. Control above the gene. Meaning, with the master's voice which is the mind or consciousness. The scientific term is, "The Master Voice." So the genes are subjected to the mind the way your mind thinks. As you think, so are you! Science and God's written Word are one. Science with every discovery are proving every single written Word of God.

Jesus was talking about *epigenetics back then. Gene control has been debunked by proving embryonic stem cells morph to their surroundings causing them to change.* Again, proving that you can break generational curses from Exodus 20:5, Deuteronomy 28:1–68, etc. This is why God says that you curse the generations to come even unto the fourth generations. He is talking about habits, people!! Stop over spiritualizing it!! Stop doing the things you know are toxic!!!

You consist of fifty trillion cells!! And each cell holds 1.4 volts of electricity. Now times that by fifty trillion cells, that is seven hundred trillion volts of electricity! Definition of *electricity*—a form of energy resulting from the existence of charged particles (such as electrons or protons), either statically as an accumulation of charge or dynamically as a current. We consist of negatives and positives just like a battery does. Placebo and nocebo—positive believes in something that will heal you while nocebo believes that something will kill you resulting in it happening. The blessing, placebo, positive electrons, or protons to be proclaimed on Mount Gerizim and the curses,

Self-Power Is the Great I Am

nocebo, negative electrons or protons to be announced on Mount Ebal (Deuteronomy 11:29).

Today you choose between the positive world that exist just as real as Mount Gerizim or the curse that is as real as Mount Ebal. Every cell in our body has minus voltage on the inside and positive voltage on the outside like a battery.

Bruce Lipton is an American biologist who has proven that gene expression can be influenced by environmental factors. He is a genius, in my opinion, along with Emoto and Dispenza. What Jacob did by using the sticks, water, and the marking on the trees are very scientific (Genesis 30:25–43). Dr. Masaru Emoto proved the same thing by using water and words, and Bruce Lipton proved it with blood changing or transforming based on environment. Joe Dispenza has proven it by your thinking, feelings, and beliefs. When you change your thinking, you heal yourselves and can heal others. They have proven again all what God specifies. We're made of water! Dust minerals! We're made of seven hundred trillion volts of electricity.

Really, God's glory and spirit equaling His breath He blew into Adam's nostrils that created first chosen genetics. No wonder words and beliefs can change the cells which simultaneously change us. We electrically change our own body of water and also have magnetic pull to ourselves also known as law of attraction which, in fact, is God's Word that says we can ask, believe, and receive. He will do exceedingly above all that we think, ask, and imagine!

Bruce Lipton has proven thoughts are not in our heads. They are outside of your heads. God says to take thoughts captive and bring them into the obedience of Jesus Christ. I will elaborate more with coordinating scriptures that are compatible with science in my volume 2 of *Self-Power Is the Great I Am*.

Why a gazelle knows that a lion is not their friend miles away? Because they can feel the energy or a bird to a cat. Energy can be felt. Be sensitive to vibrations, auras, and vibes. Spirit is what Jesus calls it. All organisms communicate by vibrations. We connect with vibrations; the energy is felt. We are interacting waves. We study the waves, not the particles. We're atoms, but we are also the field.

In magnetoencephalography (MEG) and electroencephalography (EEG), you put wires on your brain and read the brain activity. In MEG, the probe doesn't even touch the head! You can read your brain activity outside of your head. God talks about the prince of the air and spiritual battle and to not be tossed or turned by winds or waves, literally energy waves and winds of thoughts.

Take every thought captive. Take it captive from where? Up in the air and bring it into the obedience of Jesus Christ. Thoughts are not contained in our heads. People are not particles. They are waves, and waves get entangled with each other. The people that you get connected to, you are entangled with. Just thinking of something you literally connect yourselves to—it's people, places, things, etc. When someone shatters a glass with their voice, this is called harmonic resonance or constructive interference. So we are the ones that create the feelings or signal, and when we create that signal or signals, we then send out waves that will connect to the things that can make our thoughts come to pass so just like sending the right frequency that will cause the glass to break. What glass will break or respond to your magnetic wave? Same with out of the abundance of the heart, the mouth speaks. It's an indicator of what waves you are releasing when God says life and death are in the power of the tongue. It's literally magnetic waves that are magnetizing the things that you think causing your core belief system to manifest in your quantum world.

MEG key word is *magnetoencephalography*. You are the magnetic signal by what you create, and you are attracting things to your magnetic field of thoughts or cluster of thoughts. Your thoughts and judgments are not just connected to you; they are connected to the people you think about and same with the things that you think about. They are literally connected to them. So if you think negatively of someone, then they will send negative thoughts or talk negative about you. The curse returns to where it comes from. God says don't judge so you won't be judged because you will send off that magnetic vibration. Nikola Tesla proved energy can power things that are not physically touching the power source. It is important to know that we are like ocean waves, and when a negative wave from a different ocean is coming our way, we will then feel that wave of negativity; however, that is when we must create from within positivity so we can counteract that negative wave.

Bruce Lipton, I quote, "Stress is the number one cause for diseases and common factor for all cancer patients." Cancer is not a gene. It is created through stress factors; that is a fact. There is no gene that causes cancer. When we release stress, it is a toxin called cortisol that shuts off the immune system. When we are angry, fearful, sad, depressed, hopeless, or restless, we are releasing stress equaling to cortisol that is slowly killing us. Actually, that is why our immune systems are not at its PAR level, and we catch a cold or flu more easily. In fact, cortisol is so effective that doctors give patients doses that are about to receive a foreign tissue such as a new kidney, heart, or lung. Cortisol shuts off their immune system so that their body won't reject the foreign tissue.

Cortisol causes the blood in the viscera, the gut where maintenance of the body and healing comes from all the organs. It causes the blood vessels in the gut to shut down while forcing all the blood to the arms and legs. Because you are in fight or flight or survival mode, the energy is forced to where you need it as if you needed to survive and fight dangerous environment or a dangerous person or thing. Viscera is for growth, and arms and legs is for protection. And if I shut off viscera, I shut off growth.

We have to support growth because we are constantly shedding billions of cells and needing to replenish those lost cells with new ones.

Theta is the hypnosis state of mind. You watch others and family. What's your hypnosis that your conscience has to work with? How are you programmed? Conscience is the effort to change you and all your cells. Subconscience is programmed because it's been programed of repetitiveness, resulting in generational curses like God said. You have the electric charge or power to change you, which changes your offspring.

What else can science prove from the Bible for the unbeliever such as heavenly things? Neuroscientists believe that if you can think on a higher frequency, then you can change your genetics. They think there is unlimited frequencies to think on that you could transform, teleport, along with healing—which teleporting was done in the Bible by Jesus Himself and the apostles including Enock and Elijah who never died. So no new thing done under the sun here.

God says we have all power over the enemy, and whatever we put our hands to do, we will prosper. And He says that whatsoever we ask in His name and believe in our hearts, we shall receive. He will do exceedingly and abundantly above all that we could ever ask, think, and imagine. That is mind-boggling ridiculous... Unbelievers and mockers call us Christians fairytale believers, but the funny thing is they are the ones that are practicing our beliefs, our God's commands, wisdoms, and truths. So they are the laughingstock and hypocrites. Don't sit there and think that I'm not walking in love because I'm laughing at them. Wisdom herself says she will laugh at those that don't listen.

God says seek and you shall find, so individuals who are seeking for healing, money, answers, and so forth will eventually find whatever they are looking for, especially if they're putting their self-power to work. God's word is His promise, and you better believe because He doesn't break His promises. He is bound by His Words. He is not a man that can lie (Ephesians 3:20).

Now to Him who is able to do immeasurably more and exceedingly above all that we ask, think or imagine according to His power that is at work within us. Remember Acts 2:17, "In the last days, God says, I will pour out my Spirit on all people." My point here is that anyone that practices meditation, whether they believe in Christ Jesus or not, are going to reap the results that they are putting their focus on. Why? Because every creation of God is powerful! Every individual is literally pulled out from God Himself, so they are made with His glorious and powerful genetic makeup. These are godly laws. Ask, think, and imagine, and He will do exceedingly above it all for us. Yup, even if they're an atheist or a Satanist, if they practice self-power, there will be levels of power released. However, they are not more powerful than a Christian that knows their authority and power, and no, not just to cast out demons, heal the sick, and raise the dead. It is more than that becoming an absolute new creation in Christ Jesus and changing your mind from basic living to abundant living! That's why Jesus died and conquered hell and the grave and gave us the supreme authority—again, must be using self-power. Jesus came to give us life and life more abundantly.

We're to do things such as heal ourselves, including to be financially very well off to bless and prosper our family, ourselves, our neighbors, and ones in need. You're walking in a curse if you're in poverty. God became poor so that you could become rich. God owns the cattle on a thousand hills. The *wealth* of the wicked is *stored* up for the *righteous*. Poor in spirit doesn't mean financially broke! For ye know the grace of our Lord Jesus Christ that though He was *rich—financially wealthy* (Proverbs 2; Corinthians 8:9, KJV)!! Yet for your sake, He became *poor—financially broken*. So that by His *poverty—financially broken self*—you *might* become *financially rich and wealthy*! Notice it says "might," meaning, if you don't hold yourself back mentally, you might become rich too!! If you can't provide for your family, you're only lying to yourself and being in pride, not willing to change your current occupation to better yourself.

The Bible talks about an individual that cannot provide for their family is worse off than an unbeliever and has denied the faith. If you're in poverty, you are not manifesting faith to change your reality by trying something new and guess what? There are some wicked people or unsaved people who actually are providing very well for themselves and others, and they are better off than you financially. This says all of this in 1 Timothy 5:8. See, people/some Christians want to blame God for their poverty without taking responsibility for their own choices and actions! God talks about the lazy person, even the person who doesn't invest or multiply and calls them wicked for burying their wealth and talents. You may want to argue with me and say, "Well, that's incorrect. Every day, I work really hard and that's not lazy."

I say to you that the laziness falls with you not being willing to change occupations if you're financially broke and indebt. I've known people to work up to four jobs at a time and still be broke. They just do more of the same type of job, and they are so stressed out and, well, killing themselves. Have you been doing the same exact routine for five plus ten years, reaping little to no results and, yes, including financially? Then try something new! Why are you continually shaking the same tree that is not dropping any fruit! Give it up! God is not telling you to stay there! In fact, Jesus Himself cursed the fig tree because it didn't produce any fruit, and He said in another scripture that if something doesn't grow by its third year, cut it down. It's just common sense to change. Western Christianity sometimes lies to themselves thinking that lack and stubbornness is somehow Holy. News flash: it's not. It's downright disobedient! That thing is not your provider; you make the choices, and God will bless you! Love your fellow brother or sister in Christ, and I love you enough to wake you up. Because when your way up there in age and have not changed your poor non-advancing habits, you will have regret.

I walked by the field of a lazy person, the vineyard of someone with no common sense! I saw that it was overgrown with nettles. It was covered with weeds, and its walls were broken down. Then, as I looked and thought about it, I learned this lesson: a little extra sleep, a little more slumber, a little folding of the hands to rest, then poverty will pounce on you like a bandit; scarcity will attack you like an armed robber (Proverbs 24:30–34)!

A little more excuses not to change will end you up in financial lack. The laziness and constant turning of your face away from truth that you rather sleep or ignore the correction because you don't want to listen to what the teacher is teaching. You rather close your eyes to it. You're here to add to the body of Christ by not being lazy. You're very important now. Get it? Do that thing that you know you're supposed to do! The non-lazy person is not stressed out, and to everyone else, they actually look like they're barely working. It all starts with changing you and do something new!

God says in His written Word to keep busy for you don't know in which way the blessing will come. You'll find this scripture here: "In the morning, sow your seed, and in the evening, don't let your hands be idle for you do not know which will succeed, prosper or if both will succeed and bring profit" (Ecclesiastes 11:6).

He's saying, "Baby, try it all. Keep working and changing, working and changing. Advance yourself and skills, apply for the jobs that intimidate you, and be bold and confident to do something new. We live in an age an era that is wonderful to live in! Travel, change, bless someone, and be creative!"

When it comes to healing yourself, this one is actually the least effort physically and the most effort inwardly or spiritually, and well, to me, the most fun because you learn yourself. You learn what you're angry about, and you learn to change the anger by letting it go because it's killing you. God says to be angry and sin not. Meaning, hey, you're going to get mad! But you don't need to stay mad.

Science says anger is stress, and stress is the thing that breaks your body down including your mind. You learn what you're sad about, and you can stop the sadness by declaring to yourself that you will protect your precious self by not permitting sadness to reign in your loins ever again. And if it seeps in you, check that pitiful killer and get rid of it immediately! You're special and wonderful. Forgive yourself! Be loving toward yourself! Be a protector of yourself. Stand up for yourself from yourself. Notice that you are the only one that can self-destruct. Nothing or no one else can do that to you. God is your shield and glory and protects you from all harm. If evil has prevailed at a time in your life, it's most likely what you feared the most, and notice the power you release in fear is the exact manifestation that you experience. Be full of wisdom but don't be fearful.

Awful things happened to me as a child, and it was my parents' ignorance and immaturity in God that resulted in an awful childhood because they couldn't hear His voice in warning them and in wisdom. I have no ill will toward them; however, it's important to mature and use wisdom in my own life regarding my family and to teach others that you must be led by the Spirit of God. Not in a freaky way but in your own powerful way that you hear God in your heart for yourself, that you pay attention to His voice in your life, and that above it all, you let the peace of God empire your heart and His written Word confirms what your hearing in your heart and mind. That you test every voice, and if you're still uncertain, you ask God to show you another way that will make sense and will liberate you with answers or confirmations.

There's been countless times that I have tested God in a way that He respects such as I think He's trying to tell me something.

So if the message seems a little bit unclear or in pieces or I'm not catching God's drift, I will say, "Dad, can You show me again if this is really You or confirm it with signs and wonders?" Feeling peace that is a stamp of God's signature, approving the message, sign, or wonder.

In 1 John 4:2 is where you can find what I'm elaborating on. Understand that He's the best Dad ever and, man, He loves us! We're His beloved! And if we have some questions about things we are not understanding, ask and keep asking so He can help you understand. He is called the great Counselor and Helper alongside and Teacher!

4

Misconceptions Dispelled, Meditation, and Self-Power

I feel the need to shine light on Job because so many Christians today, even the messages coming out of megachurch buildings, don't have the correct input on this scripture, and God gave it to me about seven years ago. It has always bothered me not just with this story but with many of the scriptures that people have misinterpreted them and have taught these stories so wrongly, leaving the body of Christ unsure of God and leaving God's body at war with itself.

I want to shine light on some misconceptions because many, many, many Christians and unbelievers look at this story of Job and think God had to hurt him before blessing him or that it was God's will to hurt Job so much. Others think that Job did not have enough faith. All these analyzations are wrong. First, let's go to the scripture Job 1:1–5. There was a man in the land of Uz whose name was Job, and that man was blameless and upright and one who feared God with reference and abstained from and turned away from evil because he honored God. Seven sons and three daughters were born to him. He also possessed seven thousand sheep, three thousand camels, five hundred yoke pairs (so really, one thousand oxen), five hundred female donkeys, and a very great number of servants. So that this man was the greatest and wealthiest and most respected of all the men of the East (northern Arabia). His sons used to go (in turn) and feast in the house of each one on his day, and they would send word and invite their three sisters to eat and drink with them. When the days of their feasting were over, Job would send for them and consecrate them, rising early in the morning and offering burnt offerings according to the number of them all; this is the next very important information from this scripture. As a man thinks, so is he! For Job said, "It may be that my sons have sinned and cursed God in their hearts." Job did this at all such times!

At all such times, at all such times! I'll say it again—"at all such times." He was frantic, and Job did these sacrifices constantly at all such times you could say that Job suffered from paranoia because he feared so much that his children had sinned and that they would suffer the consequences. Understand that what you fear comes upon you because your self-power is creating the reality—as you think, so are you. Now back to the spiritual laws of God, what you allow as your meditation whether it's good, bad, evil, or godly and whether it's how you see yourself in the future or how you see yourself now, it's endless. What you're constantly thinking about, will eventually happen. Job 3:25 states, "For what I fear comes upon me." God, being the righteous Judge, permits Satan to actually take it easy on Job! God commands Satan that he can't take Job's life. This is mercy! Stay with me! So many people get very confused here on how could God allow Satan to kill all of Job's family and Job lost everything financially! Some would say, "What was all the sacrificing for then, God?"

In fact, God did all that He legally could do. Job permitted it! I'll say it again. Job permitted the evil that manifested! When you're doing the right things with the wrong heart and meditation, you're going to fail. Job did all the appropriate sacrifices all the while being paranoid and really, in fact, not even believing that his sacrifices were good enough or all of his sin offerings covered his family enough. That's why he did these sacrifices (at all such times). This was most likely consuming his entire day every day. Job putting his power to such paranoia actually gave full permission to Satan to have access to all that he was afraid of. Job had wrong zeal. Romans 10:1–3 explains the wrong zeal. God is the same yesterday, today, and tomorrow. Don't sit there and tell me that Job had an excuse to being paranoid because it was the time of the law or give an excuse about Jesus not

Self-Power Is the Great I Am

being crucified yet, so there was no grace. When in fact, Jesus is the Lamb slain before the foundations of the earth. *No excuse.*

Honestly, there was more power happening in the Old Testament than there was in New Testament with newer Christians... Why? Because Christians got lazy! We had ridiculous power of God demonstrated through our forefathers in God that magicians tried to compete with us! Talk about witches' curses. They don't compare to Egypt's curses that manifested through Moses, not even today! Christians in New Testament still expected for God to do everything! That's why the handful of apostles kept charging the people to wake up and use their God-given powers! They acted like Paul was a god, when in fact, he was ridiculous in meditation and, of course, faith and knowing that all the power he had was God's power that he could put to work!

Job is responsible for the fear and paranoia that he could have put an end to. Not God and not Satan. Satan has been stripped of all his power, leaving us more powerful than Satan and demonic spirits. God does not have the power to change you unless you change yourself. He can't without your agreement! He would then be a forceful God. Why do you think He didn't force Moses to speak to the multitude? Even though He commanded Moses to be His mouthpiece and Moses should have listened to God in this because Aaron let the people participate in disgusting and shameful sin!

God cannot override our power to choose, our will, our love, and well, anything. Think about the fall of man... God didn't stop them. Don't believe me? You could right now, in this moment, go out and sin, and God could not stop you! Why do you think God commands us to do so much? Because we have the self-power to do it! It was not that Job didn't love the Lord or believe in Him or reference Him. Job was consumed with paranoia. In 1 Peter 5:8, it states, "Be alert and of a sober mind." *Mind=meditation.* Your enemy, the devil, prowls around like a roaring lion seeking for someone to devour. Don't be devourable!

Satan was waiting for Job because he had seen how much fear he had that soon Satan could make all his wishes or meditations come to pass. God's hands are tied in this moment, and He has to be the righteous Judge that He is that if you're not in faith, you will have your meditations come true—good or bad! Many Christians all over the world expect God to heal them when He gave us the healing to heal ourselves! How, Jybe? I'll tell you... Faith! Let that be your meditation, not fear! How can you release such power? Getting to the secret place (Psalm 91)!

Meditation is so powerful that you feel power and you can get so filled in the Spirit that your body heals! Oh yes, I have scripture for all of this! You must reach a high place or higher frequency or realm. Higher than all of your reality! That high calling in Christ Jesus is this higher frequency that God has allowed neuroscience to discover for themselves because it's always been right here in God's written Word, power of being filled with His Holy Spirit (Micah 3:8, Exodus 35:31, Acts 2:4, and Romans 15:19 and countless more). Please study yourself, or I'll have pages of scripture references if you expect me to do all of your homework. Plus, I have to get my baby daughters to bed.

Zechariah 4:6–7 is talking about not by might and power but by His Spirit, says the Lord. We can't physically fight the spiritual world, so it's not by might nor by physical power but by His Spirit living on the inside of us. Greater is He who is in us than he who is of the world, and we can do all things through Christ who strengthens us! Did Christians miss the "we can" in this scripture? We can because of *self-power* (Philippians 4:13).

This self-power is for anything we desire—anything. And as long as it's lovely, just, pure, and of good report, He will answer the meditations, prayers, petitions, imaginations, healing, and so on because we have complete inheritance to all the riches of our God! This is why Jesus said greater works will you do. Why Jesus said all you have to do is ask, believe, and receive? The horrible thing is that if we are having no control over our minds like God commands us to, we can't do anything! He says an unstable person in all of their ways should not expect anything from the Father! It's not God's fault; it's yours! Control yourself. Gather your loins! Shake off fear! Be confident! Stop being silly! Stop listening to the loud, confusing, burdening, and depressing thoughts!!!! Those thoughts are not your thoughts! Your thoughts are lovely, just, pure, and of good report! What you're allowing to play over and over in your mind is a lie that you keep paying attention to and believing with all of your heart, so then there you are confused, broken, and powerless! Hey, but be of cheer!!!! You don't have to believe in the things that are making you uneasy and this way! Believe in truth. Every single word of God proves true! He can't lie, so you can be so confident in every promise and every truth!

You may say, "How do I stop being fearful? And how do I stop believing a lie?" Just stop! Quiet yourself down! Breathe! And breathe again and calm yourself down. Listen to the small still voice which is God. Get quiet and close your eyes! Looking forward into the black of your eyelids, taking every thought captive, or better yet not allowing yourself to think of anything. It takes practice, but get quiet and get above your fear.

Stop it! You don't have to let your feelings run you or your imaginations run you!! God gave you that power. It's self-control. Now use it! God says in Proverbs to practice self-control including many, many more scriptures of self-control throughout the Bible. Understand that God couldn't command us to do anything without us having the self-power to do so; this is common sense.

I tell my daughters to calm down when they're acting crazy and ridiculous, and they calm down because they have that God-given self-power to practice obedience, self-control, and to change their mind and create their focus on something new that creates a mood change. And so do you! Once you have passed the quiet stage for a little and you feel quiet in your body and at peace, now it's time to really start getting higher to that high calling in Christ Jesus. Begin to let go of any offenses and hate because it's not for you; it's killing you. Get to a place of thankfulness and joy and the beauty of life, not thinking of the negatives that may exist but thinking of the good and being thankful for it and falling in love with it. Imagining what you want and becoming it and having it in your imaginations that now your heart is healing and can see hope.

God says in Proverbs 29:18, "Without vision my people perish, you have to have a vision of your future so create one, anything!"

Jybe Yvves

Understand that by you creating is actually God in you both willing and acting in you to accomplish His great purpose (Philippians 2:13) for your prosperous hopeful life (Jeremiah 29:11).

When my daughters draw a picture, I'm not there holding their hand and drawing it for them; it's their imagination, and I'm so very pleased with it! God is pleased and proud with whatever you create in your heart and mind to rid yourself of the old self! In fact, God says that when His children understand everything, inside of Him celebrates!! Here's the reference, Proverbs 23:15–16.

First and foremost, anything you create is wonderful to God, and He will bless it and determine your steps, so don't worry about how it will get done. Just dream about it, and as long as it's not of blatant wickedness, feel free to create, baby! As you focus on new things, old stupid lies lose power! Why? Because your self-power is no longer threaded through the negative thoughts anymore allowing them to manifest! Negative thoughts bring sickness, and well, good thoughts bring healing! Both and all kinds of thoughts have power because your power and energy goes to them. Why someone would say, "I just feel so powerless sometimes," due to a topic or a thing happening in their life? Even the subconsciousness of an individual knows that they either have power or missing power. When in reality, they are either putting into action their power or they're not.

Why do you think God says to stay close to His words, truths, understanding, knowledge, wisdoms, and commands? Because they bring life to all of your flesh and life to all your sinews (Proverbs 3 and 4)! You then will have the mind of Christ (1 Corinthians 2:16) and all of your footsteps are ordered of the Lord (Psalm 37:23) and your able to now accomplish it all! Now you can manifest all those beautiful spiritual gifts that you long for so much because you have quieted yourself and meditated above the chaos to seek Him and guess what? You're going to find Him!

The whole Bible is like 75 percent about a spiritual world that talks about paths that are lighted by God's Word. A spiritual battle, a spiritual armor, and these spiritual things affect your real or quantum world. God is talking about pure meditation when He says that we don't war against flesh and blood but of principalities and that we must be taking high-sounding ideas and thoughts including imaginations that exalt themselves above God. Well, how do you think we're supposed to take a thought down? Are you going to take it down with your hands? No, you're going to take it down with your mind!

My very handsome and wise husband supports my book 100 percent because it is only glorifying God and destroying misconceptions of the Word of God! He gave me this wonderful scripture that is describing meditation in its purest form.

> Let your eyes look straight ahead, and your eyelids look right before you. [So close your eyes and don't let your eyes move all around in your head, focus them, and look straight forward while your eyelids are closed]. Ponder the path of your feet [think about where you are as a whole—spiritually and physically and mentally—and where you are going in life]. And let all your ways be established [now to establish your ways, that means creating solutions and making them solid mentally]. Do not turn to the right or the left. [This doesn't mean physically, of course, as I'm chuckling inside. It means to stop looking over there in your mind for an excuse and over toward the other way in your mind for distractions and etc.] Remove your foot from evil [because it's common sense! Evil is destroying you, killing you, and robbing your abundant life!]. (Proverbs 4:25–27)

Distractions are like little foxes that spoil the garden (Solomon 2:15). Catch for us the foxes, the little foxes that ruin the vineyards, our vineyards that are tender and in bloom. This means that if you're in a fragile state of mind and emotions, then you need to catch those little foxes, catch yourself before letting yourself get distracted during meditation. Foxes represent misbehaved and unlearned mental habits—how you are mentally is how you are outwardly.

I'm not saying that God doesn't do anything for us. What I'm saying is that He already has done everything for us. Now it's our responsibility to use our God-given power to become just like Him. Yes, every Christian should be practicing the laying on of hands and healing should be so easy to turn on, and it should be easy to turn off depression or frustration or fear because it's a skill and it's powerful! Honestly, these things in the Bible are considered basic teaching. Therefore, dear brothers and sisters who share in the heavenly calling—thoughtfully and attentively—consider the apostle and high priest whom we confessed as ours when we accepted Him as our Savior namely Jesus Christ (Hebrews 3:1). Thoughtfully and attentively consider these things. Meaning, meditate on it!

Therefore, just as the Holy Spirit says, "*Today if you hear His voice, do not harden your hearts* as your fathers did" (Hebrews 3:7), you must be hearing His voice in meditation through your heart. Stop closing it!

Please read the scripture references yourself. I'm using my takeaway on these scriptures!

God promises that you won't enter His rest. His rest is everything you need to flourish with long abundant life (Hebrews 3:9–11). Yes, in the quantum world and in your eternal spirit today, you need this rest/meditation. He says clearly that our forefathers tried testing Him, and well, He withstood their testing. Meaning, they tried to enter His rest and His promises in their own nonproductive way, and God said no. It doesn't work that way. It's not physical rest before spiritual rest; it's spiritual rest first and always and that comes through meditation! In fact, this angers God. How stubborn we are when we stay unlearned! So God swore an oath that we will never enter His rest doing it the way we want to instead of God's ways.

God says for us to encourage each other in the truth, which I am doing today, God calls having an unbelieving heart a wicked evil one. Why? Because if the heart has no belief, it's filled with evil and idle thoughts of wickedness that makes someone stressed, frustrated, angry, etc. (Hebrews 3:12–14), concerning these very spiritually mature things to enter rest and fullness of long healthy life through our Lord Jesus Christ (Hebrews 5:11–14).

Self-Power Is the Great I Am

You Christians today have stayed like infants in this area and are still having to be taught this elementary teaching of how to access your God-given self-power to manifest all of His truths and commands. You're so tripped up on basic teaching that you barely understand what I just said.

By all means, can we move on from the common sense teachings such as of saying you're sorry for sins and acts that lead to death and can we stop teaching about faith in God already (Hebrew 6:1)! We know these foundational teachings already. You should be far, far above these first-grade level Christianity teachings! For God's sake, come up higher to higher thinking! Operating in power of thought because power of thought is powerfully working regardless even without you having control. That's why you end up being the way you are day in and day out! You constantly need megachurch teachers to teach you instead of you teaching yourself. You by now should be teaching others considering the time you were first taught about God. Megachurches are for the lost. Are you lost? No! Those teachings are for the babies in Christ Jesus! Concerning all of this I have much to say, but it's hard to explain because you don't meditate; therefore, you are sluggish in your hearing and have come disinclined. Because you keep having to listen to other teachers and being spiritually fed infants milk, you are unskilled in the Bible and doctrinally inexperienced. Solid food is for the spiritually mature—who is spiritually strong with meditation of the things of God and whose senses are trained in meditation by practice to distinguish between what is morally good and what is evil.

This is, in fact, being holy and having the mind of Christ. We ourselves are transforming from the old person and becoming a new person in Christ Jesus (2 Corinthians 5:17; 1 Corinthians 13:11; 1 Peter 1:15).

God is needing us to see things, and by seeing things, we must meditate; and by meditating, we are using our God-given self-power that is powerful because of Him! Understand that we are knit together with all the things pertaining to God and God Himself! My daughters are me! You can't tear me apart from them because their makeup is me and them! So their characteristics are mine and theirs because they have been knit in my womb with everything of myself, absolutely everything!

When someone says, "Well, you have the heart of your mother or the passion like your father," that's more than DNA. That's spiritual. That's mental transformations to one to another! So we as humans are this way to our heavenly Father; we are just like Him. We are, in a sense, Him. We're powerful just like He's powerful because we are knitted with His power, so it's us and it's him. You can't tear these two apart! Or you're asking for a bloodbath within the individual! You are ripping the person's makeup apart! *A Christian's self-power is theirs and God's combined!!!!!*

How can God say, "I'll make 'you' strong," all by Himself? For He has to make "you" strong. Don't forget the "you." Otherwise, if "you" were not any part of self-power or strength, then He may as well do it all by Himself. Could I then say that the things that my daughters do that are obviously just like me? For example, they both hold so many attributes of myself. My youngest is very, very witty and learns super fast, and my oldest is very organized, wise, takes her time with pretty much everything, and loves to be clean, and well, all of these characteristics came from me. Do I, as their mother, take credit for what they just did? Or what they do all by themselves came from themselves with their own creativeness?

The answer is both. *I take credit because they wouldn't have that about themselves if I were not their mother. And I give them credit because they did do it themselves and with their own creativity or spin on it. We are the same with God. We have self-power because God has self-power and we have to take responsibility for it and He receives all of the glory!!! We're made in His image. We're His offspring become holy like He is holy and have His mind! Christians in a sense have become politically correct and it's causing them to put their God-given self-power down, and God is saying to us, "My children, want Me to do everything for them when I have given them the power to do it!"* Jeremiah 1:12 says, "The Lord said to me, '*You* have seen correctly, for I am watching to see that my word is fulfilled'" (Italics mine).

It's crucial that we use our self-power to see what He needs us to see and do. God asked Jeremiah, "What do you see?" God would

Self-Power Is the Great I Am

have seen Jeremiah as being a lazy person to not put an effort to see what He needed to see. In order for Jeremiah to see he has self-power. Jeremiah will see what he wants to see with his own eyes and perspective and that could be good or bad. God can't and won't change that. He freely gave us the gift of self-power, and that's why we govern this natural world the way that we do. Which in fact is why since the beginning of time, we have always had some people that want wickedness and some that want holiness, and we are warring with each other which is and has always been part of the kingdom of God that suffers violence and the violence are taking it by force.

We are God's power. Meaning, self-power. You can't separate it! These things are two yet one! Self-power is ours and God's! Working with His Power (Philippians 2:13), for it is God who works in you, both to will and to act in order to fulfill His good pleasure. You can't separate the two! Can you separate The Father, The Son, and Holy Spirit? No, of course not! Yet they are three different beings yet all God. Do they have their own will? Yes, and it's to will after what God wants.

Jesus could have said no to crucifixion. He asked the Father if there was another way to save mankind because He was terrified to be separated from God in that moment of becoming the sin and evil of this world that the Father had to turn His face from Him. Jesus knew that there was no other way even though He was terrified, which is showing you He has a free will and power to think and to ask the Father this question. You see, suicidal people that are not terrified to die, they see it as glorious or they are head first to dive into self-destruction. Jesus was not that way. He was terrified, but He channeled His mind to focus on the greater picture of saving all those that will call on His name. He is our Lord and Savior!

How did Jesus channel His mind in the garden of Gethsemane on the Mount of Olives? With self-power! Matthew 26:39 states, "'That is not my will but your will, Jesus." Jesus had a will and has the self-power to obey or disobey; however, Jesus absolutely loves the Father because He Himself chooses to do so. If God created a robot to come down here to do what Jesus did, it would not be a sacrifice.

Question: Do you love God because God is making you love Him? Or do you love Him and do all that He asks of you because you have that God-given free will and self-power to do so. I'm pretty certain you said you choose to do so. Well, if you did, you just used your free will and self-power to initiate that decision-making. Understand again that one using their God-given self-power without acknowledging Jesus as their Lord and Savior, they can't be given eternal life and they can't cleanse themselves from sin and can't make themselves pure of heart. Scripture reference: Proverbs 20:9 states, "Who can say, 'I have cleansed or kept my own heart pure; I am clean and without sin'?"

You see, not confessing Jesus as your Lord and Savior is sin itself. You see though that when you do receive Jesus, you're now the righteousness of God Himself, and you are now responsible and must become perfect as He is and holy as He is, having now the mind of Christ! Perfect is humility, admitting when you're wrong. The world's definition of *perfect* is having no flaw or error or blemish. God loves a broken and contrite spirit. One that realizes their wrong and changes, then you are becoming more like Him. Holy perfection is humility!

5
Training Senses with Self-Power via Mediation

Adolescence, I believe, is the most crucial time for one to seriously learn the voice of God for themselves. If Mary and Joseph did not hear God, they would have not preserved baby Jesus from the demonic king who wanted Him killed. Story after story, even today, of miraculous encounters and miracles that have favored the individuals in their lives and the lives of their loved ones with blessing instead of a curse. No one is perfect, but we can make the efforts to get better! Not by being closed off to people but to the toxic characteristics that we must deal within ourselves because we have a fallen nature or flesh, and those toxic people around us, we must distance ourselves from.

Yes, change. Find a new job, if you must. Rent a new apartment for a different scenery and surrounding or buy a house. Change your hair for a new look that you and only you can pull off and look as unique as you only can. You're the only you! If you're currently living with the same old job and living in the same old home that you have lived at for years, all the while sporting the same old look that you have had for ten plus years or since you were a child, my goodness, it's time for a change!!! Hey, but by all means, if you're feeling a 100 percent and your old ways are letting you feel absolutely amazing, then hang on to the past and never evolve and experience something brand-new in your life. But if you're feeling pretty down and out, it's time for a change!

Jybe Yvves

God changed the names of His sons and daughters in the Bible. He even gave them a new look at times. Saul to Paul, Sarai to Sarah, Abram to Abraham, and Moses started rocking an older and wiser look and, well, very suitable for leading a multitude of six million. The white hair, I assume, gained him much respect! Keep in mind that they didn't have amazing hair stylists like we have today!

God says wash your face and comb your hair and put on your finest. He says put on your pearls! God is robed in majesty. He is the one who created beauty. Sure, beauty is not just outward appearance, but my goodness, if you are causing sore eyes, change! Wash up and brush your hair and teeth. How you look outwardly is always a mirror image of how you feel inwardly. Your body is the manifestation of your spirit in all levels. Why must people take God's Word and try to make it impossible to obtain or act like Jesus was a turtle who lived in a shell and never lived and enjoyed life? That is what Jesus came here for, for life and life more abundantly, not more, sorry.

God wants us to enjoy our life to its fullest with family and friends, helping and encouraging others doing new things! Why must Christians have such a guilty conscience when God, in fact, said that it's your own convictions that condemn you, not his! So stop condemning yourselves!

> They show that the requirements of the law are written on their hearts, their consciences also bearing witness, and their thoughts sometimes accusing them at other times even defending them. (Romans 2:15)

Guilty conscience robs you from living life to its fullest! So stop it!

In 1 Peter 3:1–6, your beauty should not come from outward adornment, such as elaborate hairstyles and the wearing of gold jewelry or fine clothes. Rather, it should be that of your inner self, the unfading beauty of a gentle and quiet spirit, which is of great worth in God's eyesight. Stop before you take this out of context! Next, you won't be able to brush your teeth, shave your legs, or smell nice! My word, people don't understand God's Word because they don't know Him personally! It's a very sad thing that religion has taken these simple common-sense scriptures and have turned them into this enormous and ridiculous condemning silliness!

The book of Peter is simply stating that, of course, makeup, hair, and clothing do not make us beautiful. We're beautiful for our hearts and our inner being of being healthy and whole spiritually! But my God, He's not saying that you can't wear makeup and do your hair and wear jewelry! Condemnation does not have the heart of what the Bible is saying here at all! Religion has done enough damage to people and hurting of people that they can't live without feeling condemnation for everything. God sent Jesus so that we are free of a condemning curse! I've known some people with plain clothes and no makeup and a bun in their hair with some of the ugliest personalities. So obviously, not wearing makeup has not helped these people with beauty because it doesn't matter about makeup. It matters how you are!

My heart is to dispel religion but to keep God's Word! Notice that 1 Peter 3:4 is talking about inner self, unfading beauty of a gentle, and quiet spirit. It's all about your inner being and spirit, your heart, your meditation, your self-power to understand that the meditation of your heart is huge!

God says, "Above all else, guard your heart with all diligence for it determines everything, all the issues of life flow from it and it determines the course of your life" (Proverbs 4:23).

This scripture is talking about us humans meditating. The idea of meditation has been passed down for centuries. Understand everyone has access to meditation and the idea of it first was God's, so no one else, no other religion, can take credit for it. To meditate outside of the acknowledgment of Jesus Christ, God, and Holy Spirit, plus all the fruits of the Spirit, you will fail eventually. Individuals who meditate and practice self-power without Jesus as their Lord and Savior and God their creator, they won't be able to do meditation successfully without Him.

Please pay attention!!! Self-power is not demonic! This is very important to know! And God loves you so much that He appreciates your heart to obey every single word of God, but when there is very big misunderstanding, God will address it because He says in all your getting, get understanding. Self-power could only be demonic if it came from Satan and guess what? He can only take away, steal, kill, and destroy! He wants Christians to never acknowledge their self-power because then they cannot complete all of God's commands and promises!

Don't you know that you can't be saved and receive Jesus without your self-power to say that you want Him? And it's your self-power that chooses to fall in love with Him!! That it's your self-power to love Him and forgive yourself and love yourself and to love and forgive others. Don't you understand that when you give God permission into your heart, that is your self-power saying that you let Him in!! If you didn't have self-power, you would be a robot, a machine, or programmed to love and receive Jesus. Don't you understand that self-power is how we had the fall of man and don't you know that self-power is how we had the second Adam who is our Lord and Savior, Jesus Christ, who willed Himself to be crucified? Don't you know that it was Mary's Self Power who permitted God to give her Jesus by the power of the Holy Spirit!?

In Acts 17:28, it states, "For in him we live, move, exist and have our being! As some of our poets have said, 'We are his offspring.'" If we are His offspring, we are like Him for He has declared that we are made in His image. God has a free will and so do we. That free will is our self-power! It's our God-given makeup! You do everything right now in your life with self-power! Yes, He is the one that gave it and created such power in us; however, it's ours to use as we have a free will and that's why we have so much evil ruling in the world, and Christians need to understand that Daddy wants us to grow up and understand that we have to do some things on our own because He already gave us success!

You don't need to ask God for healing; you heal yourself. He gave you the power to do so. You can meditate on your body being whole and imagining it and believing it because God says whatsoever you believe in your heart. He will do exceedingly above all that you could ask, think, and imagine! He needs you to put to work your self-power to meditate on the promises of God!!!!! Then you will see the goodness of the Lord! Not sitting their hoping that you will see a move of God. Jesus told the man to pick up his own mat! That man had to use self-power to do what Jesus said (John 5:8)! When God commands us to do something, it takes him and us. Co-man-did=two men did.

For thirty-eight years, this man sat there, and you would think that, my goodness, he would figure a way to scoot himself there and stop wanting the pity! Jesus didn't care if he was needing healing… pay attention! Jesus said, "Do you want to get well?"

The man gave an excuse!

And then Jesus said, "Get up, pick up your pallet, and walk!" Jesus didn't go pick the man up, and He didn't carry the mat for him! The man did it! Self-power! Jesus, in fact, I believe was fed up with the man and charged the man with a frustrated kind of voice like your mom would say to you like, "You better get what I asked of you done." Looking at you with a kind of face that you know she is like, "You're capable!"

Having the mind of Christ and being of one faith and one spirit and becoming a new person and changing your thoughts to His and transforming into the new person…

Psalm 19:14 states, "Let the words of my mouth and the meditation of my heart be acceptable in thy sight, O Lord, my strength and my redeemer!"

6

We're This Powerful Because He Is in Us

There are many gods, rulers, and kings in the earth. It does not mean that they're the one and true living God. God says that He is the King of kings and the Lord of lords. Understand that He's talking about the three kinds of lords and kings that He is supreme over. First type of kings that He is over is all children of Himself. We are kings that govern ourselves and the world. Second type of kings are the ones that rule over a multitude of people, and lastly, the demonic ones. The lords that He is Lord over are either human or demonic. Referring to the false gods and worldly kings that try to stand against Him or above Him, God says there is no God that is beside Him or before Him because they're only beneath Him.

We're here to take dominion over the earth and be good stewards over ourselves and help mankind. We're here to rule over the enemy and keep him in his place and to pull down all high-sounding nonsense. No other god has given of himself in this way—none! Some people think that God sent Jesus on a suicide mission, and that is simply not the case. Jesus had the heart of the Father. Imagine wanting to be reunited with your family, your loved ones, and that you knew that the only way to do that was to rescue them. If you had a loved one that you could see again or set free from captivity, would you give your life? Well, this is all that Jesus did, and He knew He would be raised from death to life again to be reunited with us all. The beautiful thing about it all was that when Jesus decided to go through with the perfect escape plan for mankind to be made 100 percent free from sin, shame, guilt, and death was that it all was decided in Jesus's heart to be our Lord and Savior for each and every one of us. By Jesus's decision from His free will and self-power, He gave us that free power and access to be reunited with our loved ones that have passed on into heaven because we will eventually be caught up with them.

Understanding that when Jesus died, He created a gene pool that imprinted death to sin, to hell and the grave. And when Jesus rose from the dead to life, He added to that gene pool power that when we receive Him as our Lord and Savior. We are in fact now made up of new genetics physically when we transform our mind like Christ.

Romans 12:2 states, "And be not conformed to this world, but be transformed by the renewing of your mind" because you will change into a new person when you think differently. That you may prove what is that good and acceptable and perfect will of God, allowing us to truly have more power than our outer world or quantum world—greater is He who is in us than he who is of this world. We are the genetic makeup of God. Other religions or belief patterns will say that the universe blesses them which is silly. The one who created the universe and universes and dimensions is the one who blesses them.

But you do have to give them credit in the fact that they are attracting blessing, and we know that it is from God. God is not a respecter of persons. His laws are in motion. Ask, believe, and receive, and He will do exceedingly abundantly above all that we could ever ask, think, or imagine. Understanding that God's laws can't change just like the law of gravity and the law of no gravity laws of magnetic fields, the laws of anything without oxygen—almost everything dies. Without blood, we die. The list of laws goes on and on…

All these laws that God has created of the Spirit and, well, if he has laws in place for our earth and outer space and our quantum world, you better believe He has laws for our spiritual. Laws of forgiveness, laws of receiving Jesus, laws of not receiving Jesus, laws of whatsoever we believe we will have, laws of asking anything in His name and it shall be done or the simple acknowledgment that you create, meditate, and imagine because of our Lord and Savior, then these laws take place so we have unbelievers that are tapping into heavenly or God's spiritual laws that are having His promises come to pass in their live to a degree because keep in mind that these are laws. Biblical definition of *law* is what you sow is what you reap, or what you put in, you will eventually get—negatively or positively.

There are spiritual laws that He gives without sorrow, and guess what unbelievers are operating in the gifts of the spirit without acknowledging God, Jesus, our Savior, and His Holy Spirit. You cannot separate God from His Spirit or His son from Himself. And you may say, well, how is this possible that unbelievers are accessing the laws of God? Well, because God is a man that can't lie, and He is no respecter of persons and gives the gifts with no sorrow that where this scripture says in Matthew 7:21–23:

> Not everyone who says to Me, "Lord, Lord" shall enter the kingdom of heaven, but he who does the will of my father in heaven. Many will say to me in that day, "Lord, Lord have we not prophesied in your name, cast out demons in your name, and done many wonders in your name?" And then I will declare to them, "I never knew you; depart from me, you who practiced iniquity or evil!"

I healed in your name, but God will respond that He never knew you. In fact, He will say get away from Him. If He has professing Christians that are doing these miraculous works and He says to them to get away from Him, how much more will He give no attention to the ones that deny *the faith and His son, Jesus,* regardless of their miraculous works, achievements by meditation, and their God-given self-power that they want to not give glory to where it is due which is our heavenly Father. Understand that if you have professing Christians doing miracles, that disappoint God, or have no personal relationship with Him, you better believe there are unbelievers doing miracles and raising the dead and still not knowing God.

What humans put their hands to do with white hot pursuit, equaling their energetic power will magnetize their imaginations to themselves 100 percent all the time with real manifestations? It's the inevitable! God is not receiving us into heaven based on the unavoidable, ineluctable, sure success of businesses, empires, or miraculous even magical happenings that come from us. Just because all that we do prospers, that's not what makes us accepted by God! It's our raw relationship with Him. The good, the bad, and the ugly! Man, we are real children to a dad!!

Just the fact that we received Jesus Christ, we are ready to go! We can operate in all of the goodness of God and abundance of Himself. We can operate in our God-given self-power with the fullness of God's riches and glory and His voice in our life and guidance, and most of all, most of all, His love! Children must have their Father. We all came from our biological fathers' seed. Whether or not he was a real father to us or not, we come from his seed—simple.

Mankind must have their Creator. If you are one that is operating in self-power and meditation without acknowledging that your God-given self-power comes from God Yahweh, you will stumble and fall. You can go so long before you can't anymore. I guarantee it because God said it. Apart from Him, we can do nothing. He says that we plan our plans, but He determines our steps. In Proverbs, He says that so clearly you can imagine and meditate and use your God-given self-power, but eventually, God will determine your steps with or without you. How awesome would your God-given self-power and meditation be if you would acknowledge God? How much more secure would you feel? How much deeper would you go in the things of God?

Enoch never died. He disappeared and was caught up with God. Famous neuroscientists today say that if we can create a high enough frequency to think on, we can definitely transform or live forever because if everything we think of and believe comes true, our genetics will mimic what we think and we can have those miraculous signs and wonders. News flash: it's already been done. It is in

Acts 8:26–40 regarding with teleporting and in Genesis 5:24 and Hebrews 11:5 regarding with never dying and transforming. People want to argue this. God always confirms His Word in at least three or more mouths or ways. It says in Matthew 18:16, "But if they will not listen, take one or two others along so that every matter may be established by the testimony of two or three witnesses." I'll take a few scriptures from the written, very proven, Bible as my two or three as to confirm that this indeed was teleporting and transforming.

More regarding on transforming and teleporting:

> The Transfiguration. Six days later Jesus took with Him Peter James and John the brother of James, and led them on a high mountain by themselves. And His appearance changed dramatically in their presence; and His face shone with heavenly glory, clear and bright like the sun and His clothing became as white as light. And behold, Moses and Elijah appeared to them, talking with Jesus. (Matthew 17:1–13)

> The tombs were opened and many bodies of the saints who had fallen in sleep in death were raised from death to life and after the resurrection of Jesus the Saints that were raised entered the cities and appeared to many people. (Matthew 27:52)

Regarding with never dying includes our great example, Jesus Christ being raised from the dead with His glorious transformed body that passes through walls, yet His disciples could touch Him clearly, not being a ghost, being flesh and not having blood. Jesus Himself before His crucifixion transformed on the mountain of transfiguration, including Jesus giving us eternal life. The list of outstanding stories with Lazarus and so on confirm that it already happened, and neuroscience is acting like they discovered something new. God doesn't need us dead to transform us or give us eternal life. Jesus did all that for us! He conquered hell and the grave! If it's conquered, then those that have tremendous faith can certainly transform!

If we think on that higher calling and even if we're promised 120 years, there are people that can head home early by being so incredibly close to God that they can transform. Enoch and Elijah had tremendous faith that they tapped into by their God-given self-power. It is in 2 Kings 2:11 when Elijah is caught up in a whirlwind on a flaming chariot and is taken to heaven. Me, personally, I don't want to transform unless my daughters and husband are there to witness it because I want to be there for my husband, children, grandchildren, and so on. God clearly gives us promised years to 120 years of age, or you can transform if you're on a higher frequency in that high calling in Christ Jesus. To me, it's all good. We all will eventually be with our Lord and Savior. High calling is high frequency—we're called to think above our genetics—also known as epigenetics. This means above the gene.

Science is equipping unbelievers to have the same results as Christians when it comes to miracles, but they can't give you eternal life, and if they can, it won't be in Christ Jesus, and there's only a heaven and a hell. I believe that God loves His children so much that even when an unbelieving individual dies, God meets them and gives them an extra chance to receive Him. But understand that God won't force anyone to love Him. Man, I know I would do that to my child if they were far from me!

God says that if a wicked parent knows how to give a good gift, then how much more does God know how to love His children even the ones who were far from Him? We have heard countless stories of those that have died, some unbelievers and believers, that have seen God and then came back to life. Also, we have proof that in some cases, they were pronounced dead and spoke of a God encounter when they awoke. God has been showing Himself to mankind in endless ways. To be an unbeliever in these days, you would have to be really silly. It's accurate how God actually calls unbelievers blind and lost like a lost little puppy, really.

Unbelievers have to know that God already showed Himself in human form which was Jesus, and they crucified Him. Don't you see that was God working His son's death out for the greatest good? Jesus wasn't supposed to die. But God knew that He would do the greatest thing ever in history and save His son including mankind by giving us all the self-power over the enemy and supreme power and authority over all of His craftiness. God is not going to send Jesus down again to be killed. Instead God has shown us His endless universe and frightening planets and endless heights and creation on the teeniest level to the grandest.

An unbeliever is simply a fool to not see God. And to physically see God with our human eyes, we would burn up from His glory. Just try staring directly into the sun with eyes wide opened directly into it. Let alone the other suns that make our world's sun look like a teeny tiny dot. Many times in Old Testament, people couldn't touch the ark because it would strike them lifeless. Our human bodies are old fashion, that is why we need to get transformed either by dying first to receive our glorified bodies. If there is a perishable body, there is an imperishable body. If there is a natural body, there's a spiritual body. He will transform our lowly body to a glorious body just as we have been born with the image of a man of dust. We shall also bear the image of the man of heaven (1 Corinthians 15:42–49; Luke 24:39; Philippians 3:20–21).

7
This Past Year Has Flown By!

My mother who was diagnosed with an incurable tumor that was cancerous passed away twice. She passed away the first time in Sacramento, California, while on hospice early April of 2018. My little brother raised her from the dead. She was stiff as a board, and you could not move her arms because they were so stiff. She was lifeless, and well, my brother shared the story with us, all the while smoking a cigarette and a few cuss words and beyond exhausted. My baby brother handled so much of everything during this time. He was the one that administered all of her medication and was her power of attorney. My brother is so incredibly strong. What he went through during all of this was tremendously difficult that honestly some humans don't have the courage that he showed on all levels regarding my mother until her actual passing from earth to heaven.

He said that when she passed, he immediately was furious with the enemy and began to rub his hands all around her legs and arms and was weeping in anger and sadness and was passionately saying he will make her name famous and that the enemy will not leave his mark this way on her life and was demanding blood to flow through her body again and that her body to operate with oxygen, and sure enough, she woke up!

There were seven other individuals that witnessed it all as well. Me and my half sister and brother-in-law were driving from Bakersfield, California, to Sacramento, California, while this was taking place. I was able to see my sweet little mother the day after her resurrection. I was able to play her favorite worship song for her, which is Rick Pino's, "Doves Eyes." She was with us for almost three more weeks and passed away late April. After her resurrection, she was then traveled by hospice from Sacramento to my eldest sister's home in Fresno, California, where she had her last days on earth. There were so many little finches that lined the fencing outside of her window. She didn't pass onto heaven until my little brother's birthday passed. It was as if she knew, and she knew she wanted to celebrate one more birthday with him on earth. My husband bought a birthday cake, and we sang it with her around her hospice bed and made a little family video.

The power of God is within us, and it takes our self-power to dive deep and pull it up from deep within us. To deny what I just stated, as a child or a human of God, you are denying your God-given gift that makes all that God asks from us possible for us to actually accomplish. Frankly, it's a complete shame and puts you in a state of laziness and infant-like faith. God calls us to a high calling in Himself. God commands us to put away childlike things. He commands us to cast off every weight! He is saying for us to do it!!! He is not doing it for us! We don't have to ask for what He already has given us. We can do it ourselves because He gave us the power to do all that we need to do to be whole spiritually, mentally, and physically. Understand that *everything* that *you accomplish or receive from the grandest to the most simple due to meditation is in fact all coming from God because He loves us. Every good and perfect gift comes from God* (James 1:17).

Our mother lived a very, very hard life and was a single mother that with all due respect, she didn't change her habits of thinking that led to depression and fears and phobias that even with being a Christian, she was not operating in her self-power and dominion to subdue the thoughts that were tormenting her. She, for years, had been saying that she wanted to go home with the Lord and that there was no purpose for her to be here on earth anymore. Life shouldn't be something that you want to escape from! Life should be full of thriving life because we get to create with time and God Himself! We can change what needs to change. There's nothing holding us back except ourselves and negative feelings that are not real. We say they are real so then they become real in our lives, but we are supposed to be managing ourselves! Out of the abundance of the heart the mouth speaks, life and death are in the self-power of the tongue. Christians, wake up! You're lazy if you think that all you have to do is confess Jesus as Lord and that is it! You're letting His death and resurrection be for nothing in your lifetime on earth if you're not enjoying and evolving in this beautiful world He has given us.

I know God, my God of whom I fell in love with eleven years ago who has commanded me to write this book to prove every single word with His Word to the Christians that you have *self-power* that He has ordained and appointed to you so that you can live the life that He gave His all for. You were knitted in your mother's womb with this self-power and this uniqueness of being the only you (Jeremiah 29:11).

I remember that while my mom was at UC Davis Medical Center in Sacramento, California, still waiting to see if there was some kind of options left for her, before she went on hospice and before she was resurrected, I told my husband that he had to watch the girls and I needed to go pray. I asked a very big question that I knew God would answer because I know my Father's voice. I had the strongest faith like you wouldn't believe I encouraged my mother with all of my might. But I felt God drawing me. I sat in front of my window while the sun was shining in on me with tears in my eyes, not because I didn't have faith but because she didn't have faith anymore. Proverbs 18:14 states, "The human spirit can endure in sickness, but a crushed spirit who can bear?" I asked God if my mom will live or will she die. He responded to me with, "That when she is alone at her apartment, she cries out for Me to take her." I wept because I knew her will to die was her wish, not God's, of course. But she created a reality of her inner desires. Her will to die was very much stronger than her will to live.

Jybe Yvves

Understand when you hear from God, you also must understand what the spirit is saying

1. God was making clear to me that my mother's desire was to pass away and head to heaven, not necessarily in sickness but somehow some way, and because of how depressed she was, she created the very thing that answered her will, not God's. God's will is for a long satisfied life, latter days to be far greater than our former days. *The wages of sin are death. The wages of missing that high calling or mark in Christ Jesus lead to death.*
2. He was saying that because of this strong desire and depression, she has caused herself to become sick. *Let me make it very, very clear. God doesn't make His children sick. Sickness comes from ourselves with negative emotions running rampant within us nonstop that in fact, God commands us to stay away from all evil because He knows we're fragile when operating in darkness that we seriously deteriorate. And we have all been born into a broken nature, so there's possibility for health problems when coming from the womb if the mother and father lack operating in epigenetics by believing God's promises. The mother and father should always be interceding over the mother's womb in confidence and not in fear because what you believe, you will receive. We must be able to heal, and that's why it's so important to use self-power and meditation. Also God will guide us in all things, so it's crucial to have a close relationship with the Father who can direct your paths. God is an experience, not an explanation.*
3. He allowed my mother to be raised, of course, to show us that His will was for her to live! Not to die.

My mother's strength of being a single parent and that nothing ever made her quit or stop providing for her children was what has made me thoroughly tough and strong, yet God is what has taught me to love enormously. Her strength physically was what led me to believe she had strength spiritually, and that was not the case.

Self-Power Is the Great I Am

She wanted to go home with the Lord. She would have long conversations with my little brother, and she was so full of thoughts that were depressing that only broke her body. God told me that He raised her the first time she passed to demonstrate that it wasn't her time but that she would head home early because she will have the desires of her heart because her heart and mind asked, believed, and well eventually, she received. It was what she longed for so much that she created a reality. Be aware what you're saying and thinking because wishes and fears can come true because your power is demanding them. Faith and fear both require you to believe in something that does not yet exist in the quantum world.

Side note: Job's fear summoned Satan to the courts of God. In fact, Jobs fear demanded Satan to do all that he feared. Remember how I said that God told me that I was choosing the very thing that I was fighting. I was so afraid of what I chose to make real when in fact, my fears never existed until I chose to believe my fears were real. And I said that there was something that God needed to deliver me from when in fact and in truth, none of my fears were real and I was believing a mirage or a tricky imagination of a thought pattern. God never needs to deliver me from anything. He already has delivered me from it. I only need to get myself on the frequency of believing that anything that I'm fighting or fearing is a lie by creating things in my mind that bring me happiness, newness of life, and change of thoughts, then my inner being and cells and body will organize itself, resulting for me to not operate in fear anymore. God says to forget those things which are behind me and to press forward into the high calling or frequency to change my focus and power.

Usually when someone is physically sick, they most likely are emotionally not well. That's just how it is. We're not made to strive in darkness of our minds but thrive in life and light of our minds.

I remember three years ago, I was experiencing depression due to some goals that had not been obtained and just being at home every single day doing the same things day in and day out. I was and still am a stay-at-home mommy. When we're not healthy emotionally, we affect the ones around us. They feel our negative emotions, especially our children. We must understand we release thankfulness and joy and peace right now, not when the house is cleaned and the dinner is done and the things you want to purchase are purchased or whatever you may be hoping to get done in order for you to feel complete. Feel complete now, then do the things on the list, all the while feeling peaceful thankful and joyful.

Before my mom's diagnoses, my oldest daughter was four years old and was diagnosed with a ruptured appendix on January 2018, four months after my youngest daughter was born and all the while dealing with depression. Sometimes as parents, we can't even identify depression because we are always on the go. The wonderful and most powerful thing is that in my weakness, God guided me with such wisdom. Before the doctors diagnosed my daughter, it had been two weeks of appendicitis. I told them, and they kept bouncing me from hospitals and misdiagnoses. I kept returning to the emergency with my newborn and husband and my four-year-old, Satori, who had not properly used the bathroom in days, including urinating.

We finally were admitted when they said that here in Bakersfield that their CAT scan machine was down and that they had no specialist that knew how to operate on a person under forty pounds. Doctors were finally saying that this could be appendicitis, and I remember running to the bathroom in emergency and screaming! I was all over the place emotionally, and then I gathered myself and began to declare truth and complete anger toward this evil influence over my daughter's body.

She was laying on a gurney in the emergency hallways on IV. I walked up to her and began to rub her little face that was so pale, and she always called herself rosie posie. I felt like I was physically fighting for my daughter against someone that was trying to kidnap her. But it was all spiritual and emotional and with health issues. I spoke over her in power and commanded her rosie posie to return to her, that all of her blood cells would be penetrated with the blood of Jesus, and that every cell in her body to be made cleaned and resilient and would then subdue the thing that was causing her to be made sick. I was imagining that as her cells beneath her skin was in chaos would be in obedience to my voice to be made well again. Where fear tried to seep in with my husband, I was his encouragement by

Self-Power Is the Great I Am

declaring life and healing and creating an atmosphere of confidence that she would be just fine because the enemy is a lie and is simply not the truth. I wouldn't walk mentally, and during my meditation in that room with her in fear but in confident hope, when I would feel the spirit of fear I resisted it or thoughts that created sadness, I refused to think in them. I was using my self-power to will what I wanted to meditate on. And well, I had it after forty minutes to an hour of loud declaring and confidence, my daughter sat up and asked me to help her use her potty. She had not gone bathroom in days. We had to take an ambulance ride from a Bakersfield Hospital to Valley Children's Hospital in Madera, California. The fog was so incredibly thick that night, but my husband drove with our newborn as I drove with our oldest in an ambulance ride. It was a process and months in the hospital and weeks of intravenous antibiotics and draining of abscess and ultimately the removal of my daughter's appendix on April 10, 2018, and my mom's passing in late April 2018.

Yes, to have these two catastrophes happening simultaneously was absolute hell, all the while having my little newborn living in a hospital with us was creating enormous stress. Financially, we were so impoverished as well. Our sunshine was our Selah, my little newborn who even made Satori laugh throughout her long stay in the hospital. And when Satori was first admitted with a ruptured appendix, my littlest stretched out her chubby little arm and hand to Satori and she held her hands, and it truly was that Selah knew her big sister was experiencing pain and wanted to show love toward her.

While there was such joy after a long four months that our Satori was better than ever after all that, the focus moved to my mom being on hospice and heading home to the Lord two weeks later, which was incredible in its shock and surrealness. Sitting here even now, it doesn't seem true, not one bit.

I endured a few panic attacks, including with bizarre arguments with my husband. I had to tap into my self-power to get me out of this very present and real distraughtness. I told my husband one night after a panic attack that I needed to go pray in the living room and be with God. He was a bit concerned and was wanting to make sure I was okay. I went and sat in the presence of God and played a worship song on my phone and the lyrics went like this, "You unravel me with a melody. You surround me with a song of deliverance from all my enemies until all my fears are gone." I felt every word of that song of God, accomplishing every lyric in me in that moment. I felt like all of the panic melted away, and I was clear in my mind again that I had control and that I'm solid. I'm not a silly woman. I'm a mighty woman. I know who I am. I know that I've got this and that I'm not tossed and turned. I refused it. I'm made with self-power, and if God says I can do something, I can. That in fact is God both acting and willing in me to accomplish His great purpose. You cannot separate me from Him and Him from me.

I always knew I was going to write books since I was seventeen, and well, with my mom's passing, I felt like it's about time that I do. I've written this entire book in the matter of less than two months, all the while having another book already done as well that I actually wrote after my mother's passing.

We all have stories and struggles, but we all have self-power to get beyond the storms of life because God gave it to us, and when we allow misconceptions of God's Word into our belief system that say we don't have self-power to obtain every single dream and passion including wealth, we hinder the abundant life that Jesus gave His all, including His life for. If we want our children to be best in everything and through life and to be healthy and financially well-off, why in the world would anyone think that God wants us opposite of that? In fact, to be poor financially, you actually are a slave to money instead of a ruler over it. Money will tell you, "Nope, you can't do this or that all the time." You can't bless no one because you are too busy hoping someone will bless you when you should be contributing to mankind and not taking on an endless basis.

I hope that my book helps you see that you can change your life because you have the self-power to do so! God's written Word was the first to declare it in every single aspect and God is proofing it through science today. Begin right now, this moment! Start creating mentally and change outwardly! Change your surroundings and your personal appearance to new and better!

Self-Power Is the Great I Am

Just like when a child needs to stop wearing the same outfit that is their favorite costume or princess dress, they need to change and grow up well. So do we. So do you. Change! Live! Cast off every single weight that's holding you back! You can! And you will! Remember, we are spirits. This body is alive because of our God's Spirit. When the spirit leaves this body, it's dead, dark, and lifeless. That invisible spirit is life itself. You can clearly see when that breath is gone, and life is absent from the human body. The human body that once was our familiar loved one is now foreign because you were always familiar with the Spirit, not the empty body.

So, remember that every day is super natural and breathtaking like a beautiful dream. Thank God Almighty that our life is infinitely and delicately dreamlike and beautiful and so is heaven. It's heaven on earth. Be thankful today. Love yourself. Be easy on yourself. Encourage yourself. Don't talk your spirit down. Don't leave your spirit sad. Change your perspective, and your reality will instantly change. Life is life, but if we choose to look through the lens of gratitude, the nightmare reality is just a horror film and not even real. Truth is real. God is truth. Every Word of God proves real! Live without restraint! We live forever! Eternity is what we graduate to more life, riches, and abundance with glorified bodies, and mostly, with our families forever with our Daddy forever and ever. Amen!

About the Author

Jybe Yvves is a loving wife and mother of two princesses. She has been a stay at home mommy for going on 7 years. She loves decorating for every birthday, season, & Holiday especially Christmas! She has been a passionate teacher of Gods Word for 11 years now. She chases down the difficult questions and answers with direct commonsense. She has counseled many women from all walks of life. Although she is 28 years old she has been a confidante of women of all ages well into their mature age of 80. She has lead christian women groups throughout California with powerful encouragement of knowing their purpose. She may be pint size but is dynamite for Gods Kingdom. She is not a lightweight when standing for Gods Word. She is not intimidated in the slightest when challenged on what she fights for no matter who is challenging her. She is raw and she is real.

CPSIA information can be obtained
at www.ICGtesting.com
Printed in the USA
FSHW010948240720
72244FS